The Beer Hunters

A Tale of Scottish Metal and Lager detecting

The

Beer Hunters

Craig Stevenson and John Mackay

Cheapwayround Publishers
East Kilbride

This book is dedicated to
the bar staff who put up with our
nonsense as we travelled the
length and breadth of this
great country

First Published in 2016 by
Cheapwayround Publishers

ISBN No; 978-0-9570252-6-4

Typeset in East Kilbride by
Cheapwayround Publishers

Edited by Ian Bailllie

Printed and Bound by
Bell and Bain Ltd.
Burnfield Road, Thornliebank, Glasgow, G46 7UQ

Cheapwayround Publishers
22 Balfour Terrace
East Kilbride, G75 0JQ

Cheapwayroundpub@yahoo.co.uk
www.cheapwayroundpub.co.uk

By the same authors;

The Cheap Way Round

Still Going

Going Roon the Edge

Inn Aff the Bar

Mud, Sweat and Beers

The Auldest Boozers in Toon

Contents

Ayr 12
Millport 24
Oban, Ganavan Sands 38
Dumfries (Southerness Beach) 50
Rothesay (Kerrycroy Beach) 64
Lamlash (on Arran) 78
Irvine Beach 96
Sandhead (Luce Bay) 108
Girvan 124
Portobello Beach (Edinburgh) 138
Dunbar 154
St. Andrews 170
Dumbarton-Beach? 186
Trip to the top 202

Introduction

We have been travelling around Scotland, checking out the state of the nation's pubs, for a few years now. I can honestly say that we have enjoyed every trip we have made. Obviously there have been the odd moments when we have had to endure a particularly boring bus journey or pub which has totally underwhelmed us. But for the most part we have had a grand old time travelling through the greatest scenery in the world and socialising with some truly memorable characters.

In the past we have visited coastal towns and villages, enjoyed the hospitality on offer in the bars and hotels there but, somehow, we have managed to avoid the most obvious feature of these places: their seafront: that was about to change. Scotland has some really great beaches and we intended to visit as many of them as we could.

Many years ago I bought a cheap metal detector, with the intention of finding hidden treasures and historical artefacts. Unfortunately things didn't work out that way. That wasn't because I was looking in all the wrong places or even because I was particularly unlucky. No, the main reason I failed to make my fortune was the detector I had bought was a piece of junk. It would barely register a coin if it was sitting on top of it. Fortunately, metal detectors have improved greatly since those days and we were able to buy a really good one.

I had learned that people are not supposed to just wander about digging up the countryside without permission. This can be difficult if you don't actually know who owns the land you want to search. Detecting on the beach is a different matter altogether.

Basically the beaches of this country are owned by the Queen. But fortunately, for us, Her Majesty is not too bothered about who digs holes in her sand.

The biggest problem I had to overcome was John's

objection to 'making a prat of himself' on the country's beaches. You do tend to stand out a bit, traipsing up and down the sand looking as if you are doing a spot of hoovering. But I knew that with a with a bit of subtle persuasion and a lot of alcohol I could convince him to give it a try.

Not only would our new hobby allow us to visit new areas of the country but, given we would have to spend quite a large portion of our available time out on the beach, we would be spending a lot less time propping up bars the length and breadth of Scotland. Bus drivers and the general drinking public would be queuing up to thank me for sparing them from the prospect of John's most outrageous patter.

John; There is no doubt in my mind, Craig has finally cracked! I've known him for about 15 years, and he's had his fair share of ideas that are a wee bit-how can I put this without insulting him-interesting. But this latest one about treasure hunting is mental. It's straight out of the hidden place in his mind, a mind that had its formative years in the wee Ayrshire mining village of Auchinleck.

After many pints one winter evening, he managed to talk me into agreeing to his idea of a book on Treasure Hunting. Get me drunk and I'll agree to anything. My first question on sobering up was 'what will a machine cost us'. 'They're almost giving the things away', was his all to quick reply. To be fair to Craig, he insisted on paying most of the cost as he wanted to keep the thing.

Within days he had ordered, and had delivered, a '*Garrett Ace 150'*. According to Craig, one of the best in the market and guaranteed to make us our fortune!

The only plus side of this idea is that it is completely different from our other books. All right, I will admit we are using the Bus Pass to get about, we will be taking pieces to save money, and we will be visiting pubs in the places we visit, but apart from these minor details, we are entering a completely new field-or in our case-beach, of writing.

Ayr

TREASURE
MAP
The Royal Burgh
of
Ayr
River Ayr
SOUTH HARBOUR St
A719
FORT St
A719
Firth
of
Clyde
ESPLANADE
CHARLOTTE St
L&Ms
BUS Stn
BATH PLACE
W Sq
FULLARTON St
PAVILION ROAD
W Sq
WELLINGTONS
BAR
ALLOWAY Pl

John; *The Journey:* If you have read the introduction, you will know that Craig is going to write about our experiences hunting for treasure on beaches all over Scotland, at least the ones with a pub close by, and give you details of our finds, plus anything else that takes his fancy. I reckon it's going to be a bloody short chapter.

My job is to plan our trip, get us there, and at the end of each chapter give an account of what really happened.

The reason we picked Ayr for our first beach of call was that it was the start of February, and the weather had been miserable. So we did not want to go far, as we would be coming home in the dark. Finding our way home in the daylight is hard enough in the state we usually find ourselves in!

Ayr is definitely the easiest beach to get to from East Kilbride. I think it must be the only one that you can get to from EK using only one bus, our local X16, which connects us to the Ayrshire Coast.

As usual, I walked down the hill to pick up Craig. In our previous travels, all we had to carry was our pieces, and maybe a few of our books to try and sell to cover the price of a couple of pints. But not when you are searching for treasure!

This was our first time transporting Craig's new all singing and dancing '*Garrett Ace 150*'. He actually wanted the even more expensive '*250*', but we would have needed an earth mover to go down to the depth this thing claims. I told him the '*150*' would make us look daft enough.

The device splits into three pieces for easy carrying and the instructions suggest that it can be put together by a halfwit in about a minute. We had practised for about an hour assembling it earlier in the week, so when I got to Craig's house, he was ready. What I didn't know was that he had also bought a telescopic wee shovel that's designed to turn into a big shovel. So that was something we would have to put together on the beach. I could see us returning sober today!

We got on the X16 at about eleven o'clock. We didn't have to worry about the device bleeping on the bus, because as usual, nobody was paying with cash! If it had bleeped every time a bus pass was produced, the battery would have run out by the time we left the bus station.

The driver of our bus was a wee rounded bloke who you would call a real character (hope wee rounded bloke is politically correct). Anyway, as we were approaching Kilmarnock and people started wanting on and off the bus, he discovered that he had lost the ability to open the door using the button, or whatever he pressed. So at every stop he would shout and bawl that the door, along with the indicators and other things, were not working. He would open the doors manually, shouting continually at everyone getting on and off the bus. But he was happy and cheerful, and assured us all at each stop that this was a nightmare, but he would get us as far as Kilmarnock Bus Station, then it was in the lap of the Gods.

We arrived at the Bus Station mentally scarred by this wee guy's happiness at the bus doors not working. When he parked the bus there were a couple of bus workers or Inspectors or someone in uniform standing next to our stop, so he got out and started shouting at them. They just smiled at him and one of them came over to the bus, pressed a button and the doors were working fine.

This wee guy had amazing confidence, talked happily all the time, and had no idea what he was doing. I wouldn't be surprised if he ended up in charge of transport in the Scottish Parliament. He's got all the credentials!

Meanwhile Craig, not having my couldn't care less attitude to life, was raging at the wee driver. As we arrived at Ayr Bus Station, I asked Craig if we should give the wee bloke a tip. Craig's answer cannot be printed, but it was along the lines of he wished the wee blokes mouth worked like the bus door: Permanently shut.

As normal, all the passengers, including me, thanked the driver for his help in getting us to Ayr in one piece. He had a wee speech for us all. As I said earlier, he's a natural politician. Craig said nothing!

Enough of this drivel. On to today's adventure. We got off the bus with the sun shining in a brilliant blue sky. The sort of winter's day you used to get regularly in the old days. Craig had found a pub on the web, near the beach, which he never knew existed. So that's where we headed.

Craig; *Todays Bars and Beaches.* Today was our first outing with the brand-new metal detector. In retrospect it would probably have been a good idea to do a bit of a dry run first as these things don't often go to plan; then again, nothing really does on our trips. Actually I was convinced that we were destined never to reach Ayr never mind find treasure on the beach. The bus trip down to Ayr had not gone well. Unable to turn off the engine or open the doors properly, the driver had jumped off the bus to check the outside switches. That had to be a recipe for disaster. I could imagine the headlines 'Runaway bus smashes through Kilmarnock town centre: no survivors'. I tend to be a bit pessimistic in the morning.

As usual I had done my research on the computer the night before we were set to visit Ayr. I had found a pub quite close to the beach, but given the number of pubs in Ayr that shouldn't have been much of a surprise.

I should have felt thrilled at finding a pub so near the beach but to be honest I felt a bit cheated. I have been visiting the town, man and boy, for over 50 years. When I was a wee boy, two or three day trips to the beach was the extent of our summer holidays.

Later in life I took my own family there. As was the tradition, I would get them settled on the beach with soft drinks sandwiches and sweeties before sauntering off to the nearest boozer for my own preferred refreshment. In all of those years I had never heard of or seen *Wellingtons Bar.* Yet there it was; a couple of hundred yards from the beach.

Wellingtons Bar is at the far end of Wellington Square. It is a basement bar and it blends into its surroundings so well that anyone could be forgiven for passing by without noticing it.

I think that it is quite possible that local bylaws make the owners keep a low profile given the up-market architecture of the area. Actually it is just as likely that its position so close to the Sheriff Court means that they don't really want to advertise their whereabouts as they might not fancy sharing a customer base with the court.

Wellingtons, Ayr

Every time I see the court buildings I am reminded of that old Ayrshire joke; 'what you call a Cumnock man in a suit?-the accused'.

Wellingtons Bar, once you find it, is a great wee pub. It has a really traditional country pub feel to it. I noticed that there were quite a few real ale pumps at the end of the bar which for me is always a bit of a worry; they seem to be taking over. Fortunately nobody took offence when, after checking out all the fonts, I ordered my usual pint of Tennent's Lager. I had expected to be snubbed. Right enough there were only two other customers in at that time, so it would be hard not to notice if there was any snubbing going on.

The idea was for us to have a quick beer in the pub before moving onto the beach. We had hoped that some of the customers or staff would be able to tell us about any particularly good spots to try detecting. But since there were only two other customers, I felt our chances were limited.

Our barmaid, Rosie Martin, was keen to help but didn't know of any lost fortunes on the beach.

I was checking out the pub when I overheard John asking Rosie about the state of the tide. That worried me more than a little. I had assumed that John, the man with salt water in his veins – 'I have a Day Skippers Ticket'- Mackay would have checked this all out before suggesting Ayr as our destination. Rosie said that she was fairly sure that the tide was out, but couldn't be entirely certain.

Rosie Martin, Wellingtons , Ayr

On the way down to the shore I told John about the shoaling qualities of the beach. Having over the years paddled in, swum in and occasionally fallen into the sea at this very spot I knew that the shallows extended a fair distance out from the shore. As we approached the sea wall all we could see was the sea.

We did laugh a bit, but the nearer we got to the wall the more hysterical that laughter got. The water was actually lapping up against the wall when we looked over it. That seemed to be the end of our first attempt at treasure hunting. Since neither of us had thought to bring wetsuits and snorkels, it looked like we would be back talking to Rosie a lot sooner than we had intended. Fortunately we discovered the only strip of sand on the West Coast of Scotland which wasn't currently underwater.

It was only about 100 yards long and 20 feet wide but it suited our purposes. Our problems should have been over, but I hadn't counted on John's manual dexterity, or to be more precise, his obvious lack of it. While I skilfully put the metal detector together I gave John the task of screwing the handle on to the small, brand-new, shovel I had bought to help dig up the treasure we were sure to find. He screwed it up completely. My extendable shovel completely failed to extend. In fact it didn't even manage to operate as a shovel. The way things turned out we didn't have much need of a shovel anyway.

When at last we did get to scan the small strip of sand available to us we soon heard the detector bleeping. John got quite excited at this and started digging away, like a dog after a bone. It would probably have been a lot easier for him if he had been able to use a fully operable shovel.

I let him get on with it for a while before I pointed out that the strong signal he had acquired was coming from the iron railings I was leaning against. Undaunted we continued scanning.

Eventually we did get a signal and I have to admit that we were both quite excited. There was definitely something just a few inches down in the sand. We were grinning from ear to ear thinking we had hit the mother-lode.

Instead of a chest of Celtic gold coins and jewellery our

entire haul consisted of two small pieces of a blackened material which we decided to describe as iron encrusted meteorite fragments.

John {Canute} Mackay keeps an eye on the incoming tide

It has to be said that everyone we showed our precious finds to later on were less than impressed. In fact most of them were uncharitable enough to say that they thought our meteorites looked suspiciously like two small lumps of coal.

In total we had spent about an hour on the beach and had very little to show for our efforts, but I had thoroughly enjoyed myself. I was amazed to find that John had also had a good time. So much for all his moaning! We will definitely be continuing with this detecting lark.

With the tide threatening to swamp the last bit of beach we decided it was time to get our feet off the sand and onto the sawdust of the nearest pub.

John had discovered another bar even closer to the beach and as far as I was concerned that qualified it as a place of interest.

We made our way along Bath Place to *L&M's*. I would have to say that this pub could never be described as traditional looking, not on the outside at least. Actually, I thought it was just an extension of the café next door. John on the other hand had spotted the sign out on the pavement declaring that drinks are sold in 35 ml measures. That man would crawl over broken glass to get into a pub selling what he likes to call 'real' measures.

Inside, the pub reminded me of some of those bars you see in the rough end of Spanish holiday resorts. In other words great! It was a bit dark in the bar, probably because there are no windows in the place. I nearly fell down a couple of stairs at the door. When I mentioned this to the barman he told me that on a sunny day he gets many a laugh at customers tumbling down those stairs. The change from bright sunlight to bar room gloom catches many thirsty holidaymakers out.

After a hard shift metal detecting down on the beach we were ready for a cool drink. While knocking it back we told the barman what we had been up to. I really thought he might be impressed but when he laughed I did think it was a bit cruel. He explained that the part of the beach we had been on was a favourite spot for the detectorist fraternity. He said the sand would have been picked clean a long time ago. Once we finished our drinks we made our way back round to Wellington Square. We had said to Rosie that we would be returning for an après detection drink and to show her all the treasures we had no doubt found. Luckily for us the pub was a bit busier than it had been earlier so there was no time to show off our meteorites.

Instead I got talking to the owner of *Wellingtons,* Nan O'Brian. Nan and her husband Mick bought the pub 25 years ago. Sadly he died a few years back but Nan has kept the place going strong. In fact the pub has won the CAMRA South Ayrshire pub of the year award for the last three years. The pub also does a roaring trade in lunches, especially for the workers from the many offices which line Wellington Square.

John was chatting to Rosie and discovered that her dad was none other than Norrie Martin, the Rangers goalkeeper who was with the club from 1958 until 1970.

Unfortunately this was just the excuse John needed to wander down memory lane, or Copland Road to be more precise. For someone who claims to be a Partick Thistle supporter John seems to know an awful lot about that particular Glasgow team.

One of the guys sitting at the bar must have heard John talking-it would be hard not to-and recognised his accent. It turned out that this chap, Colin Bradbury, was originally from East Kilbride and knew a lot of the people John used to work with. That was all the encouragement John needed to launch into the history of every printing company in Britain.

The upside to this was, I now had time to enjoy my pint and chat to Nan. I reckoned that, from past experience, I had at least 20 minutes of uninterrupted peace before John remembered what we were actually supposed to be doing in Ayr.

For our first attempt at metal detecting I think we did alright. Obviously we didn't make our fortune by finding any lost gold or precious stones, but we had enjoyed ourselves. And you never know, maybe someday our meteorite/coal samples might turn out to be of scientific interest.

So while treasure was a bit thin on the ground, pun intended, the first pub we found could be described as a wee gem. *Wellingtons Bar* is a very comfortable pub, ideally situated for beachcombing, and is just around the corner from the bus station.

I still can't believe that I managed to miss this pub in all the years I've been coming to Ayr. From now on this will be 'our' pub whenever we are passing through the town.

Of course I will also be visiting *L&M's,* especially on sunny days when I will take a seat at the bar and watch the tourists tumbling down the steps. As John has pointed out many, many times, I have a rather odd sense of humour.

John: ***A review of the day:*** As you have probably read in the introduction, I was not keen on the idea of the book. I can regularly make an arse of myself without wandering about on a beach with what looks like an upside down umbrella stuck out in front of me.

Having had my moan, I've got to admit that I really enjoyed the day. The pub Craig picked for us was brilliant, with great owner, staff and customers, and the searching for treasure was more fun than I thought it might have been. Craig even forgave me for not organising the tide to be out. In fact, we were worried there might be no sand at all. We were right up against the wall at the beach before we saw a wee slither of sand to search on.

I think Craig has also forgiven me for breaking the wee shovel which is now no longer expanding. Thank goodness one of us can bend down to dig out the treasure. To be honest, I don't think the bending is going to be an issue, although you never know. The two pieces of metal-filled coal-like stone that ignited the *Garrett Ace 150* might be treasure; you never know.

After a quick couple on the way back to the Bus Station, we dozed most of the way back to EK. Thank god we had a door-working bus with a silent bus driver.

Today' s finds

John's thoughts on today's finds;

The photograph above depicts our very first find, and I reckon it may be very valuable. The noise our '*Garrett Ace 150*' made when it was passed over the treasure was like the one made by the puggies in Vegas make when you win the jackpot, or so I believe. The best I ever did was two cherries! Correct me if I'm wrong, but do diamonds not start off looking exactly like the photograph above. That's all I'm saying.

Craig's thoughts on today's finds;

A small piece of totally useless stone!

How to get to Ayr Beach (by bus from Buchanan Street Bus Station)

The X76 will take you all the way to Ayr Bus Station.

From there you turn right, cross the main road and head down to the beach. You will see the old fun house which I think used to be a dance hall. It has four towers and is a brilliant looking old building.

Wellingtons Bar is on the left hand side of the road about 200 yards from the front.

L & M's is on the left as you walk away from the beach with the former dance hall on your right.

Millport

TREASURE
MAP
Millport
Isle of Cumbrae
N
E
W
S
Kames St
Ferry Rd
The Tavern Bar
Kames Bay
Glasgow St
Guilford St
W-Bay Rd
Newtown Bay

John; *The Journey;* We wanted to go to Millport as early in the year as possible. The reason was that one of the pubs which faces the main beach is *The Tavern Bar.* Craig had found out that the legendary owner of his favourite bar, Bobby, renowned for always having Westerns on the telly, and sneaking fly brandies and smokes, is planning to sell-up and head out to the prairies to herd cows and live the dream. We had to visit for a last time before he left.

From EK to Millport is no great distance as the crow flies, although it's definitely seagulls that fly to Millport! The place is hoaching with them.

Our normal method of getting to Millport via Largs, while spending as little money as possible, involves us getting the old No. 18 from EK into Glasgow and then the McGill's '*Clyde Coast Flyer*', number 906, or even the 901, which goes through Gourock and past The Cloch Lighthouse. Well worth the extra 10 minutes. Mind you, how McGill's can call a bus *A Flyer,* when it takes almost two hours to travel about 35 miles is beyond me.

A continuing complaint we have about the McGill's bus to Largs, apart from the time it takes, is that the seats have less padding than a skate board. By the time we get there, all feeling in the nether regions have gone.

As you probably know, Craig has appointed me the position of the 'how to get there' organiser. Could I find a way of getting to Largs using the bus which would be more comfy and take less than three hours?

Because of our past travels and my memory not giving up completely, it came to me in a flash that from Glasgow, we could get the X36 coach to Ardrossan, then pick up the 585 which I think goes from Ayr to Gourock. I realised that because this meant changing buses, the time to Largs would probably not be any less. But we had been on the X36 on a previous journey to Beith, and it was a lot more luxurious than *The Flyer*. I checked *Traveline Scotland*, and sure enough, the overall time on the two buses worked out almost exactly the same as *The Flyer,* but with the changeover time, it worked out a wee bit longer. But our bums would not be as numb.

I was on a roll. It suddenly occurred to me that to save the hour it took getting into Glasgow, and up to Buchanan Street, we could get the X16 from EK to Kilmarnock, then get a bus from there to Largs. On checking again with *Traveline*, I discovered that we would have to get the No. 11 from Kilmarnock to Irvine, then the No. 585 from there to Largs. The actual time on the buses worked out about 15 minutes less than the other two routes, but with connecting times added the overall time door-to-door was the same as the others-about three hours.

On the day before our trip, we had a meeting at which I gave Craig the three travel options I had so painstakingly worked out. I also reminded him that my preferred route, the one that took only one and a quarter hours plus changeover time, was the train. Now I know the train is not in the spirit of our travels (because it costs money). But we would still be taking pieces and getting pissed, so as Meat Loaf would say, 'two out of three ain't bad'.

Craig pretended he was shocked and said 'no way were we going on the train'. I reminded him that we did get a discount on the trains, especially the EK to Glasgow journey. I also reminded him that our old age pensions had just gone up by about one pound fifty a week, so we could afford to splash out a bit. We could use our extra pension money to buy a can or two to drink on the train. I also mentioned to him the sore arse part of the bus travel to Largs. I even warned him about the dangers of changing buses in places like Ardrossan and Irvine.

He was still not convinced. That is until I mentioned that all the bumping on the buses, and the continual getting on and off might damage his beloved *Garrett Ace 150* detector. That swung it! It was the train to Largs, followed by the 10 minute ferry to 'The Great Cumbrae', then the 10 minute run on the No. 320 bus into Millport. By the way, there is only one bus route on the island.

Why is it not the number one bus, and who cares! I was just happy that we were going to be travelling in luxury on the train, with the toilets and the '*you can have a drink if you like*' law.

Craig had insisted that the trip to Millport had to be on a Saturday. I assumed that as it was the winter (the start of March), the place would still be shut midweek.

Recently, I have sometimes varied from my traditional choice of pieces, but I have decided that nothing beats the corned beef, heavy on the English mustard, on plain bread, so that was what I was carrying as I wandered down the wee hill to Craig and Irene's house.

Once our pieces were transferred into the *Garrett Ace 150* carrying bag, which I carry, Irene gave us a run down to EK Rail Station to catch the 10 o'clock for the swift half-an-hour run into Glasgow. We had about 20 minutes before our Largs train time, so we got ourselves carry-out coffees for the train (it was only 10.30am after all). Craig got some fancy thing with cream and chocolate on top, while I got my usual black Americano. The thing was roasting. We were past Paisley Gilmour Street before I could have a sip. It was still warm when we reached Largs.

I love Largs; it's like being on your holidays. We walked down to the pier, and as we had just missed the 11.45 am ferry and it was a pint till the next one, I went into a wee temporary cabin to get our tickets while Craig nicked into *Charlie Smiths* to get the drinks up. Only it wasn't *Charlie Smiths*, it was called *The Three Reasons*. I had always liked the old pub and asked the barman to give me one good reason why the name had changed. Craig told me to shut up before we annoyed him.

After a quick one, we went over to the ferry and I enjoyed a couple of my pieces during our 10 minute sail over to Cumbrae. It had been an incident free journey, and this continued on the short trip on the 320.

After our first trip to Ayr, when the tide was fully in and we almost had no sand to search on, Craig had checked on his magic phone to see when high tide was today. I'm sure he said 12.30. This was fine as it would give us an hour or so in our first pub so the tide would go out a bit and give us some room. Craig, noticing the tide seemed to be a bit high, and getting higher, checked his phone again. He now claimed that high tide was 2.30pm, as he had said all along! I had my doubts! Fortunately Irene, a Millport fanatic, had told me that there is always sand to play on, even at high tide, so I let Craig believe that I believed his story of the high tide time.

So we arrived safely in Millport and headed into *The Tavern* to have a couple and ask Bobby and locals if there was any treasure buried in the sand. I will leave it to Craig to let you know of the outcome of today's adventure.

Craig; *Today's Bars and Beaches;* The journey down to Largs went without a hitch, if you don't take those electronic gates at Glasgow Central into account. I have yet to get through these things without something going wrong. Even the workers seem to have had enough of them. As we made our way to platform 13 the young girl at the barriers called us over and let us through without asking to see our tickets.

Then again it was the wide wheelchair gates, and she had spotted John causing chaos on the platform by assaulting innocent passengers with our large equipment bag. To be honest it wasn't so much the bag that was causing the problem as much as it was the long handled shovel sticking out of the bag that was proving dangerous.

After John had broken my state-of-the-art shovel on our first outing I decided to punish him by getting him a long handled kid's toy shovel to do his digging. The fact that it was fluorescent green made it even better.

Usually when I use the ferry from Largs to The Isle of Cumbrae I like to stand outside and take in the view; not this time. The weather had changed and it was really cold and windy. We reckoned that the rain or even snow couldn't be far away.

Strangely it didn't occur to us that the conditions would be just as bad if not worse on the other side of the island where we were heading. Not ideal conditions for metal detecting. Something else which didn't occur to us was the state of the tide. Although I now have an app on my phone which predicts that tides for a week in advance, we somehow forgot to consult it. The tide would be at its highest point by the time we arrived in Millport.

This was only our second trip and twice we had completely mucked things up. However a quick phone call to Irene, our Millport expert, set our minds at rest. She told us that even at high tide there would be a good part of the beach available to us. Once that was settled we decided to celebrate by nipping into the Tavern for a swift couple of beers.

The Tavern is our favourite pub in Millport and is usually the place to go if you want to know what is going on in the town. We had read in the papers that gold had been discovered in Millport and were keen to hear what the locals thought of this. I have to admit that I expected more of a reaction but the guys in the bar were less than enthusiastic about the potential gold rush. In fact it was suggested that the whole thing was a bit of a scam. Some names were suggested to us as likely suspects but for reasons of legal liability and personal safety I have decided not to name names. Bar room opinion has it that the gold rush story was created to remind holidaymakers to book early for the new season. Apparently ‘only an idiot would think that there was any truth in the story’. I have to say that I didn't like the way they were looking at us when this statement was uttered. Although, standing in the bar with a metal detector, shovel and headphones couldn’t have helped our image.

After a mere two pints I was ready to start detecting. We left the pub and crossed the road to the beach, in the sure and certain knowledge that the guys in the bar were having a really good laugh at our expense.

As promised there was a good stretch of sand for us to work.

It was very close to the famous crocodile rock which incidentally was also the site of the alleged gold find.

I began my first sweep while John stood about trying to hide his luminous shovel from passers-by. Not long after we began I got a really strong signal from the detector. John immediately forgot about his embarrassment and started digging furiously in the spot I had indicated. In fact he was a wee bit too enthusiastic with his digging. Sand was flying everywhere. Men, women, children and small dogs had to run for cover. The signal turned out to be a false alarm. Either that or with his energetic shovelling John managed to fling whatever it was I had found further down the beach, or quite possibly, out to sea.

Don't look now but there's a crocodile behind you

We had actually marked out a grid on the beach to show the areas we had scanned. The only problem was it became harder and harder to see the lines once John started chucking all that sand around.

About 10 minutes later I got another strong signal. This time

John toned down his sand shifting and we found our first item of the day.

It looked to me like a large lump of rusty metal, but John got very excited. After I cleaned away all the sand from it I realised that what we had found was indeed a large lump of rusty metal. John disagreed. He claimed that it could well be a piece of metal from a World War Two submarine.

Since we were being ridiculous I suggested that it was more likely that it came from the reactor core of the nuclear power station, just across from the beach. But he was having none of it.

About 10 minutes later I got another signal. Before he started digging again I told John that he had suffered enough and gave him the real detecting shovel. Last time we had been out John had somehow managed to break it. My revenge was to let him use the kids shovel for a while before admitting that I had in fact fixed the original one.

I really thought he would be angry about this but he was too excited to be bothered. Once again the sand was flying but I managed to catch a glimpse of an object whizzing past my head. It was a flash of gold and now it was my chance to get excited.

Just for a second those stories of gold deposits being found in Millport came to mind. I could see pound signs. The object when we found it turned out to be a small statue of an elephant, and it was indeed golden. The trouble was the gold was actually brass. Still, a find is a find.

I was quite pleased with my golden find, but I was a bit puzzled by John's reaction to it. He kept referring to it as a child's toy when it was quite clearly an ornament, probably, at one time kept in some old Biddy's display cabinet.

For John to think of it as a toy made me wonder what kind of childhood he'd had. Maybe his parents used to give him things they had lying around the house and told him that they were his Christmas presents.

It was really cold by this time and I was glad to hand the

detector over to John. We got a few more alerts but nothing came of them. I do have to admit that my joke with shovels backfired a bit. The long handled kid's shovel was much more useful than the state of the art piece of crap I had bought, although it did make a few tourists smile when they saw it.

The beach was beginning to look as if it had been used as an artillery range, with deep potholes the entire length of our scanning area. John insisted that these would fill in naturally as soon as the wind got up. I wasn't so sure about that, but it did seem like the easiest option, so I just went along with it.

In The Tavern: John displays our 'treasures'

Back in *The Tavern* we showed off the artefacts which we had recovered from the sand, but got little response. Millport folk are hard to impress it seems. After another drink or two we made our way up towards the pier. Our quest for valuables had not ended.

For one thing we were under orders to visit the town's sweetshop.

Millport tablet is highly prized by certain people from East Kilbride and to return home without a couple of slabs of the stuff could make life difficult.

We also had need of a couple of cans of beer from the off-licence for the homeward journey on the train. Over and above all of this we had one final metal detecting task to perform. Many years ago, more years then I am allowed to mention, Irene lost a bracelet in the town's small harbour. Actually as a huffy wee child she threw a bracelet into the water. Every time we pass the harbour, which is very often indeed, I have to listen to the story of how the bracelet landed in the tidal harbour. I sometimes feel as if I was actually there when it happened.

The famous Tavern Bar, Millport

My master plan was to scan the harbour with a view to finding the bracelet. Even if I couldn't find it, which was more likely, I could at least tell her the next time she came out with the story that without a doubt her bracelet wisnae in there anymore.

There is a saying about the best laid plans of mice and men, and I am very sorry to say that my plan went agley with a vengeance. Thanks to our inability to fathom out the tides we found ourselves looking down into a totally flooded harbour. The silver lining to this was that we now had some time on our hands, and we know exactly what to do with spare time. *The Kelburne Bar wa*s beckoning. We only had time for the one pint before catching a bus from the pier, but we had factored into our travelling arrangements enough time for a quick pint in Largs before grabbing a bag of chips for the train home.

As usual we split up our precious finds. I claimed the shiny statue and John opted for the lump of potentially lethal radioactive metal. I was quite happy to let him have it as I didn't really fancy risking any further hair loss, preferring to leave that up to nature and my poor diet. John, who is a lot less worried about such things, became the proud owner of a fragment of Hunterston B.

We had enjoyed another great day out and found some interesting artefacts into the bargain. I'm not quite sure what John wants to do with his lump of nuclear reactor but my golden elephant now has pride of place on the mantelpiece.

John: ***A review of the day:*** Craig had a bit of fun with me by not telling me that he had fixed the expanding, telescopic trowel he had bought. I thought I had permanently broken it at Ayr.

He had bought me a child's spade with a big long wooden handle which made me look even more like a numpty than I already am.

After a wee while, he produced the expanding gismo and even showed me how to assemble it. It's an amazing bit of engineering. You can carry it about in a wee bag about five inches square, which Craig said will fit onto your belt. I reckoned that wandering about with our *Garrett Ace 150* in hand, and an expanding shovel on your belt would make me look like Batman's grampa.

It can also be rebuilt into a pick, presumably for attacking people who ask if you've found anything. It also has a serrated edge and a bottle opener on the digging part. My point is that after assembling this engineering marvel, the thing goes from about five inches, to twelve inches long! What's the point? There might be one though, but I don't get it. But it looks brilliant, so Craig is happy.

Our journey home was very pleasant. We nicked into the wee offy in Millport and bought a few cans for the journey home. That's something you can't do on the bus. Well, we've never been caught doing it.

Today' s treasure finds

John's thoughts on today's finds;

I was very interested in the thin, interestingly-shaped piece of steel, which I am sure comes from a sunken battle cruiser, or submarine. I am looking into it further. If any of you readers have any suggestions, keep them to yourselves.

We found this toy elephant some daft wean had lost on the beach. It fairly cheered us up. The photo above shows it in detail.

Craig's thoughts on today's finds;

Finding the golden elephant will probably be the high point of our detecting careers.

How to get to Millport Beach (from Buchanan Street Bus Station)

As I mentioned earlier in the chapter, there are two ways that I found to get to Largs from Buchanan Street. (there may be more).

The first one;

McGills No. 906 (or 901) *Clyde Flyer Service* from Buchanan Street to Largs.

The second one;

Citylink X76 to Ardrossan, then the 585 to Largs.

Then get the Millport Ferry (quarter past and quarter too the hour in winter and every fifteen minutes in the summer). Takes about 10 minutes. Ferry is on the hour and half hour on the sail back.
Get bus No. 320 (check it's the right number) from the Cumbrae slip straight into Millport. Beach on left, pubs on right. Bus takes about 10 minutes.

To come home, reverse above instructions.

For EK residents only;

You can get the X16 to Kilmarnock;
Then the No. 11 to Irvine;
Then the No. 585 to Largs.

P.S. If you can afford it-take the train.

Oban, Ganavan Sands

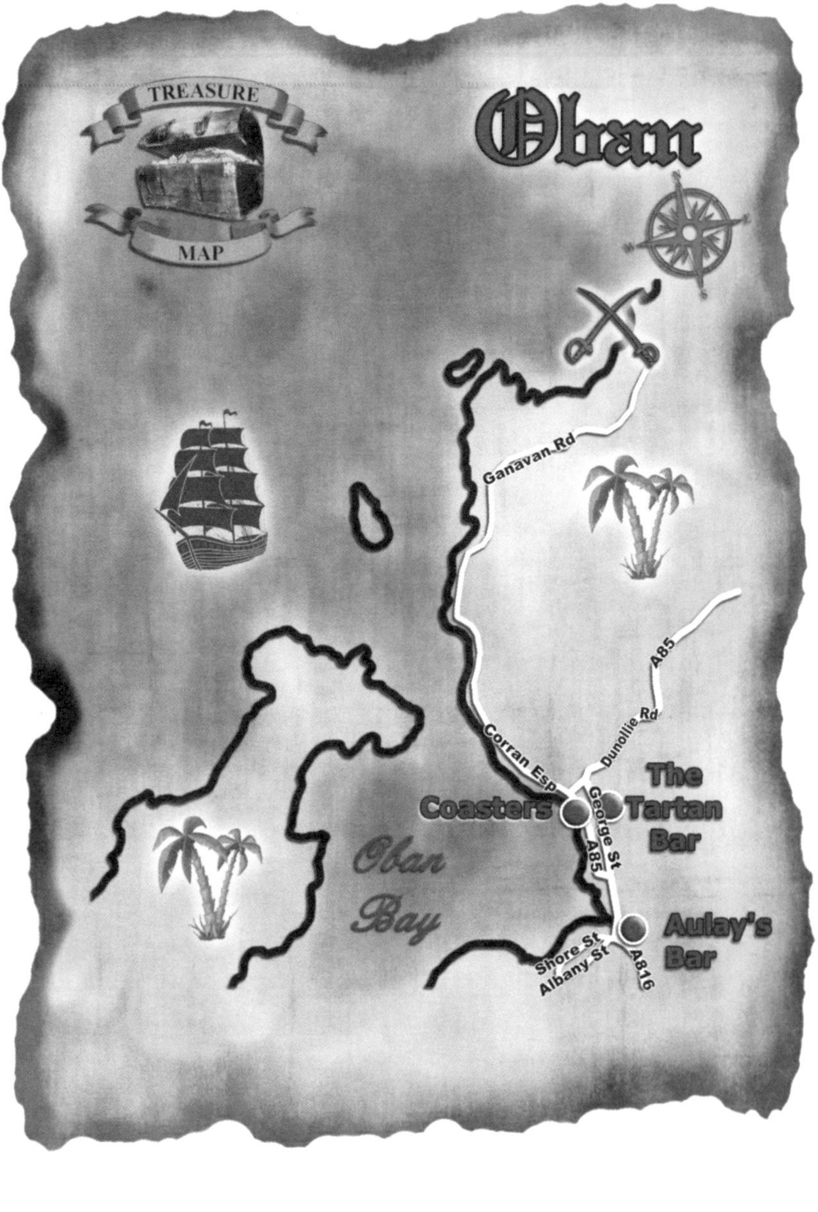

John; *The Journey;* Today's journey is one of Scotland's most scenic, taking in Loch Lomond, The Rest and Be Thankful, Inverary, Loch Awe and other wonderful places. Even I was impressed by the grandeur. I also always enjoy passing Connel Bridge, not only because it is a very nice looking and iconic bridge, but more importantly, it means you are only about 10 minutes or so from enjoying your first pint of the day.

Our coach was leaving Buchanan Street at 8.30am, so the alarm was set for 6.30am. I picked up Craig at seven and after three unsuccessful attempts, eventually got on a No. 18 bus. I'm sure Craig will slag me off about it. The thing about getting the bus this early is that there are real people on the bus going to work. The later buses are full of the oldies like us. We even heard people paying with money!

It was a lovely run to Oban. The bus went up the side of Loch Lomond, then took a left at Tarbet, through Arrochar at the top of Loch Long, then over *The Rest and Be Thankful* before stopping at Inverary, to let the bus cool down. Our dramatic driver was complaining about an overheating problem, but asked us to cross our fingers, and assured us that if we got over the hill outside Inverary, the rest would be a dawdle. Come to think on it, the wee driver who took us down to Ayr on our first trip had trouble with the doors, among other things. At least this guy wasn't completely mad.

As usual, *The Vital Spark* and the big sailing ship, which I'm sure has a name, were moored at the Inverary pier, and it was sad to see the run-down state of both of them. I am sure the locals could get together and give them a bit of a lick of paint. That's all it would take to brighten them, and the whole pier area up a bit.

We were soon on our way, and about an hour later were passing the Connel Bridge. As I was looking at the fierce rapids below the bridge, I noticed that there was a crowd of people getting into canoes. I said to Craig that they must be mad, but Craig assured me, that as an ex-canoeist with experience of rapids, the Connel Bridge set were a piece of cake. I had my doubts, although the nearest I've come to rapids is when I pull the plug out in the bath.

We left the dare-devils to their fate and enjoyed the ten minute run into Oban. The first thing we did when we alighted the bus (got off) was to deliver the books the Oban Waterstones had ordered about a week ago. You don't think we decided to come all the way to Oban just to search for treasure. Commerce comes first! After the books were safely delivered, we headed to the nearest pub to discuss with the locals where all the treasure was buried, and have a wee bevy as well. It would be rude not to.

Craig; *Today's Bars and Beaches;* It was an early start for us today but, as it turns out, not early enough. Somehow John, the man in charge of all aspects of our transport arrangements, arranged for us to miss the same bus twice. We saw the number 18 whiz past just as we came out of my front door. Then, after jumping on another bus in order to catch up with it, we arrived at the bus station just in time to see it leave. I took this as an omen. But then again I take almost everything as an omen.

We actually managed to arrive in Oban more or less on time. I was quite surprised about this, almost as surprised as our bus driver who had been predicting engine failure every time we came to anything steeper than a humpback bridge.

As I may have mentioned in the past, I have no real liking for Oban, probably because I have never found a really decent pub there. *Auley's Bar* went a long way towards changing my opinion of the town. It is a nice comfortable pub, well decorated and clean. There is even a bit of stained glass window along the front of the pub.

Auley's Bar is just like a traditional Scottish pub, only shinier. There is a bar and lounge, but since we don't usually rate lounges we didn't bother looking in. From what we could tell there is a good mix of locals and tourists. The pub is ideally situated in the centre of the town, close to both the railway and bus stations.

After a three hour bus journey from Glasgow I knew that it would be a brave but foolish man who got between John and the bar. Being neither of these two things I stood back and let him in to buy the first round of the day. As you might imagine that round didn't last very long. It might have if John hadn’t noticed that the spirit measure was only 25 millilitres. This is like a red rag to a bull for this man.

His chosen drink nowadays is vodka and soda. For some reason he thinks it is a healthy option. I could see the point of that if he kept his intake of the stuff down to a sensible level. To be honest he takes so much soda in his drink I don't know how he can tell the difference.

My only problem is that I am obliged to keep up with him, drink for drink. It would be really bad form to let him order up single drinks.

Once I had calmed him down and plied him with drink we got onto the chat with our barmaid, Kimberley Blight. Our only tactic so far is that when we enter a pub, we ask the bar staff if they know of any promising stretches of beach where we can search for hidden treasures.

Kimberley is in her late teens or early twenties and for almost all of her life she has lived in South Australia. When she spoke it was like listening to ‘Neighbours’, so I was a little surprised when John asked her if she was a local. While I accept that Oban is a fair distance from East Kilbride it did seem a weird mistake to make. Maybe the vodka was a bit stronger than he thought. We spent a very pleasant hour in *Auley's* talking to Kimberley and some of the customers. Between them they came to the conclusion that Ganavan Sands would be our best bet for finding anything with the detector. I was happy to hear that, as that was the only stretch of beach we had found on the map which looked to have any actual sand on it.

The many faces of Kimberley Blight

John, possibly with an eye on not getting too far away from the town's pubs had suggested that we find a bit of Oban's beach, no matter how small, and just dig it up. Oban beach is predominantly pebbles and large rocks and I could see a major problem with this idea. We certainly haven't stinted on getting the best quality of kit but there are limits on what we can achieve. Simply put, at one end of my detector shovel there is a high tech, case hardened, cutting tool. Unfortunately at the other end of it, all I have is John. We had no chance whatsoever of even making a dent in that beach it would take a JCB to do that.

So with our next destination settled we stepped out of *Auley's* just in time to see our bus zip past: there was a definite and annoying theme developing with our transport arrangements. However, we are rarely stuck for something to do when things don't go to plan.

The buses out to Ganavan Sands might not be too frequent but they are regular, every hour in fact. That gave us time to visit another pub before we headed out to the Sands. *Coasters Bar* is on the promenade and is conveniently close to the bus stop. My first impression of the place was not very favourable. It looked a wee bit to modern for my liking. Worse still, we could see people sitting having lunch in a raised area at the front of the pub. Had there been another pub close by I think we would have given *Coasters* a miss, but as it turned out, that would have been a mistake. There is no getting away from the fact that it was a modern pub inside, with far too much polished metal work and not nearly enough varnished wood, but it did have something going for it that we always appreciate: good staff.

The two lads behind the bar were up for a laugh and we chatted for a while, the length of time it takes to knock back two pints of lager to be precise. One of the boys was particularly interested in our search for treasure. When he told us his name was Calum that was enough for me to get my phone out to show everyone at the bar photos of my newest grandson who also goes by that name. Having bored the staff with the 20 or so snapshots I have on the phone, and finished our booze we sauntered over to the bus stop just in time to catch the No 417.

The journey up to Ganavan Sands takes about 9 minutes, but since we had never actually laid eyes on the place John was a bit anxious about getting off at the right stop. Luckily for us our driver noticed this and shouted back to us that he would be taking us right to the Sands.

Ganavan is at the end of the line for the bus which waits for a few minutes before returning to Oban town centre. Of course John's nervousness might have been due to withdrawal symptoms as I had just broken the news to him that there were no licensed premises out where we were going. You would have thought I had just told him his dog has been run over by a steamroller.

On a nice sunny day I expect Ganavan Sands is quite spectacular, it's just a pity that today wasn't one of those days. It was overcast and a bit on the chilly side. I even had to wear my gloves while using the detector.

John once again marked out a grid for us to scan and we began searching for whatever valuables the beach has to offer. After about an hour we had dug several trenches, found absolutely zero and John suggested a break for refreshments. We had bought a couple of bottles of Coke earlier in the day and although they would've been quite warm by that time it would be better than nothing I supposed. What I didn't know was while I had been using the facilities in *Coasters,* John had bought a couple of bottles of beer and hid them in our bag.

By happy coincidence my Hi Tech shovel has a bottle opener incorporated into it and we both thought it would be a shame not to try it out. It worked a treat. Suitably refreshed we continued scanning. Our bad luck also continued with the Sands refusing to give up any of it riches. Because there is only one bus an hour we were happy to keep strolling up and down the beach more in hope than expectation.

After a while we were approached by a group of people who were interested in what we were doing. We chatted for a time about Oban and the chances of finding anything on the beach. One of the guys brought his young daughter with him, and she was particularly interested in our detector. While I was talking to the boys I heard the machine's alarm go off then the wee girl let out a shriek of laughter. It seems that John had dropped a coin in the sand when no one was looking and then let the lassie find it with the detector. She was absolutely delighted.

While I was packing up our gear John suggested that it might be a good idea if we pretended that we had found a couple of beer bottle tops on the beach. He thought people might not believe we had been doing any detecting if we came back empty handed. I pointed out that since I had just taken a picture of him drinking from a bottle of beer maybe those people would be able to work out where we got the bottle tops from.

Exactly on time our bus arrived and we made our way back into Oban. It was the same driver from two hours earlier and since we had been his only passengers on the way up he recognised us straight away. Once again we had the bus to ourselves. West Coast Motors can't really be making much money on this route when you consider that we were the only two people using the bus and we had bus passes.

Our plan was to go back to *Auley's* for a few beers before catching the bus back to Glasgow. But going back to that pub would be a wee bit embarrassing after all our chat about finding treasures. As we travelled along the main road on the 417 we noticed what looked like a traditional old man's pub. I shouted to the driver to let us off at the next stop but he had obviously heard what we were up to and stopped immediately. He told us that the pub, *The Tartan Tavern,* was one of the best in town and he hoped we would enjoy our stay there. The moment we stepped through the door I knew that we would. This is no tourist pub, *The Tartan Tavern* is the real McCoy. We walked to the far end of the bar and almost immediately got into conversation with some very nice people.

Shaun Frame, Jim Irvine, Nicola Gemmell and Pat Graeham

Pat Graeham told me that she was originally from Lewis and had somehow ended up in Oban. I didn't want to put my foot in it by asking if that had been an improvement or not, but John had no such qualms.

I might have mentioned it before but it is worth saying again, John is not very good at geography. He was about ten minutes into his story about the time he had visited Lewis when it dawned on us he was actually talking about Orkney. The drink was really flowing, mainly because our new pals insisted on buying rounds of drinks, a gesture which, obviously, we had to return. Things could have gotten out of hand, but fortunately for everyone concerned we had a bus to catch. Our barman served up one last round and a few jokes before we said our goodbyes promising to return soon for another session.

Roddy Scott and John

Although we hadn't found anything at all on the beach I can say that I did find another side to Oban. I had started my day not really looking forward to the trip. Past evidence suggested that I was going to spend a boring day sitting in an overpriced hotel lounge, listening to tourists complaining about the weather. Instead we had found three great pubs and met some friendly and interesting people.

John: ***A review of the day:*** The best bit about today was the people we met and the laughs we had with them. Of the three bars we visited, our favourite was *The Tartan Tavern*, which is on the main road behind the promenade. This is a real old man's pub, the sort Craig and I feel at home in.

The treasure hunting on Ganavan Sands was not very successful, although I did find a couple of strange objects, but I'm sure Craig will have told you all about them. By the way, Gavanan is a lovely beach, and only a 10 minute run on the 417 bus from Oban pier. It's well worth a visit with the kids if you are ever killing time till the next ferry tae the isles.

As soon as we got on our bus home, the driver announced that the toilets were out of order. I'm sure he sounded pleased about this inconvenience. It was going to be my bladder that would be overheating on the way home, not the engine.

Thankfully, he said that he would stop in Inverary for a few minutes for a comfort break. I'm sure this meant we could go to the lavy. This was a three hour journey, for goodness sake, and after god knows how many drinks we'd had, I was worried.

We used the toilet break in *The Inveraray Inn* to purchase a couple of bottles of something or other to keep us going on the last leg of the journey. Obviously not alcoholic drinks as they are not allowed, especially if the driver catches you!

We were soon home in EK, no wealth of treasure, but lots of memories of a great day in The Gateway to the Isles.

John's thoughts on today's finds;

I believe we found something a very interesting today. We found that not every beach has treasure waiting to be found. But, as the saying goes, better luck next time.

Craig's thoughts on today's finds;

The only things John found on the beach today were beer bottle tops. He did find a lot of them, mainly because they were all his.

How to get to Oban (Ganavan Sands) by Bus from Buchanan Street Bus Station

The 976 from Buchanan Street Bus Station takes the best part of three hours. It's a hell of a time, but worth it for the scenery. Once in Oban, the number 417 leaves every hour for the 10 minute run to Gananvan Sands.

Dumfries (Southerness Beach)

John; *The Journey;* Today's trip was the first, of a good few I'm afraid, where we end up going to places that Craig want's to visit to relive his youth. I know Southerness Caravan Site was a popular spot for his holidays in the past. My attitude is if we can do it in a day, what's the harm in it.

We left Craig's, all tooled up with not only his *Garrett Ace 150* detector and magic expanding spade, but last week he took delivery of his latest gizmo, a battery-operated pointer that is used to prod the sand with to get an exact location for the treasure we think we have dug up. We had to carry that too. He's definitely lost it!

All this metal detecting equipment, and we couldn't detect the the approach of the big metal No. 201 bus which we were planning to get into Hamilton to meet up with the X74 which was leaving from Glasgow.

It drew in at our stop about 50 yards away and we wandered towards it (Craig can only do wandering). The driver waited till we were at the back of his bus and pulled out. What can you say? I cannot print what Craig said. An 18 arrived just after the 201 left and we got on it in the hope of catching up with it at the EK Bus Station and getting on it there (so Craig could to give the driver a piece of his mind, what is left of it). We had tried and failed with this ploy on our last trip. We failed again. Our bus pulled up at its stop just as the 201 left. Things could only get better.

I was not worried as there is a 201 every 10 minutes and had allowed plenty of time to get to Hamilton. We got there in time for Craig to go into a wee shop and buy a nine-volt battery for his new magic pointer.

When we got to our stop, there were a few people already waiting for the bus, which had started its journey from Glasgow. So Craig was on edge every time someone else arrived and stood closer to the gate than we were. We had no need to worry as our bus was a huge big double decker. Only it wasn't! When you got on there was only one row of seats behind the driver (a two and a one) then the stairs to the top deck where all the seats were.

Even Craig had no complaints. The seats were very comfy, and there was plenty of leg room. The view was brilliant as you are dead high-up and could look down on all the other road users. This might seam a bit trivial, but it's great being up high.

Our bus fairly belted down the road, except for the detouring through Lesmahagow, which is not very interesting, then through Moffat, which looks a lovely wee place with lots of hotels, bars and touristy things. Quite a few women got on, going shopping to Dumfries, and I was again amazed at the difference in their accent, expecially as we were only about an hour or so from EK. Now I'm not saying this is a bad thing, it's just amazing that in a tiny country like ours, the accents change so dramatically from place to place.

We arrived at Dumfries at about half past opening time, and after checking where our next bus left from, which took longer than it should as I had it down as a 327, when it was a 372. To hear Craig, you would have thought I'd invaded Poland. After his rant, we wandered up a wee side street to check out a pub called *The White Hart.* For some reason Craig has always wanted to visit it. Although there seemed to be a light somewhere inside, it was shut, so we went round the corner and wandered up a wee side street and into a brilliant wee pub called *The Douglas Arms* where we enjoyed a couple before going back down to the station and getting our 372 for a lovely run down the coast to Southerness.

Craig gave me a running commentary on all the places we passed, and although he knew almost all of them, the nicest place we passed was called Carsethorn, a brilliant wee village on the beach with what looked like a great hotel/pub called *The Steamboat Inn*, right on the edge of the sand. Craig was amazed and annoyed that what looked like a great pub had eluded him all these years.

During all this scenic grandeur I had some of my pieces to

get my strength up for all the sweeping, digging and pointing that lay ahead.

Craig; ***Today's Bars and Beaches;*** It has been quite a few years since I last visited Southerness, last century in fact. I didn't really think John would go for the idea of visiting my old holiday haunt but he put up very little resistance. Perhaps if he had known how many stories of my former holidays he would have to listen to he might have put up more of a fight.

The journey down to Dumfries was uneventful except of course for the obligatory mis-timing of the first bus out of East Kilbride. I won't dwell on it as it embarrasses John, the transport manager. But it's getting to the stage that if we actually caught the right bus I would expect a round of applause from the passengers.
As soon as we got off the bus in Dumfries I suggested that we should spend the hour we had before we needed to catch our bus to Southerness checking out a pub we had tried and failed to visit several times in the past. *The White Hart* is on Brewery Street and not easily found by passing tourists.

We had first tried to visit the pub about five years ago, but managed to convince ourselves that it had been closed and ceased trading. Any time we've been down in Dumfries since then we have always swung by in the hope that it might have reopened. We were out of luck yet again although I did think I saw a light on inside the pub. With the best part of an hour still to kill we decided to find another venue as quickly as possible. Just up the hill we found one which fitted the bill perfectly. It is close to bus station and we had never visited it before. That last bit could be quite important when considering where to park ourselves for a drink in this town. In the past some pubs in Dumfries haven't lived up to our expectations. That can happen to anyone but if you are then daft enough to write about the shortcomings of those pubs in a book, it might be wise not to show your face in there ever again. Happily, *The Douglas Arms* was new territory for us.

The Douglas Arms very definitely falls into the category of traditional. I would have to say that it is a bit worn around the edges but in my opinion that's a positive sign. Apart from the bar fonts I thought little could have changed in this bar over the last few decades. It even has a coal fire. The weather was unusually warm for mid-April otherwise we would have been sitting toasting ourselves next to it for the duration of our stay. As it was, we sat at the bar on a couple of fine old bar stools and chatted to the licensee, Angela Breese. She has been the boss of *the Douglas* for over 20 years and told us that it was really more like a club than a bar. There is a good age range among her customers, from young lads to old guys just like us.

Angela, in The Douglas Arms, Dumfries

John had noticed a bottle of Buckfast on the shelf of the gantry and asked Angela if there was much call for it in the pub. Apparently some of the young lads enjoy a glass of it topped up with the can of Redbull. We were a bit shocked to hear that, not just because it could blow your head off but because we don't like the idea of a good traditional pub serving cocktails. It is the thin end of the wedge according to John. The next thing you know they will be selling Sangria and Tapas.

I have to say that he was most impressed by the lack of televisions in the place. There is only one and it is tiny. Angela said that through the week the telly is only used for music but at the weekend she lets the local punters watch the horse racing on it.

There are times you just have to admire the sheer professionalism of some bar staff. Even when John mentioned that we were going to be metal detecting on the beach that day Angela didn't so much as flicker an eyelid. Dumfries as you know is quite a few miles from the sea and therefore cannot claim to have a beach. What John had failed to get across was that her home town was not our end destination.

Reluctantly we made our way back down to the bus station to catch the No.372 to Southerness. As ever there was a bit of a hiccup with our travelling arrangements. John, who must have contracted a touch of number blindness, insisted that we should be looking for the No.327 and searched the timetables posted on each bus shelter. Eventually I managed to stop his rampage by convincing him that whatever the number really was, it was going to say 'Southerness Holiday Village' on the front of the bus.

It is only a half hour trip down to Southerness and for the most part the bus travels along the A710. I happen to know this road like the back of my hand so therefore I felt obliged to inform John about all the places of interest and give him the area's historical facts. He pretended that he wasn't really interested but I could tell that he was keen to find out all he could about this corner of Scotland.

Since I knew that our first stop would be *The Paul Jones Hotel* I thought he might be interested in the story behind the name.

John Paul Jones was born in a cottage on the Arbigland estate near Kirkbeanin 1747, although it should be said that his real name was simply John Paul. His father was the gardener on the estate, but by the age of 12 young John had decided that gardening was not for him and he opted for a life on the ocean wave. He got a job on a British merchant ship and within ten years he became captain of his own vessel.

Due to an unfortunate incident concerning the flogging of one of his own crew to death, Captain Paul decided to seek his fortune far from Britain's shores, and the reach of its legal system. Coincidentally it was about this time he changed his name.

As a captain in the American navy he distinguished himself in the Revolutionary War, capturing or sinking British vessels. He even sailed his ship back to the area of his birth, raiding the estate of the Earl of Selkirk and stealing his silverware. Incidentally, after the war he sailed back to the Solway to return the Earl's property.

After a stint as an admiral in the Russian navy he died in Paris in 1792. He was eventually buried with full military honours in the cemetery at the American Naval Academy in Anapolis. American historians often describe John Paul Jones as the father of the American Navy.

I had just finished my in-depth history of the Solway's most famous son and was waiting to point out the road to Jones's birthplace when our bus turned off the A710 and trundled along a narrow B road. I suddenly had no idea where we were going. John thought this was hilarious after all my boasts about having the next best thing to local knowledge of the entire area.

Things got even worse when we reached the village of Carsethorn. For one thing, I had never heard of the place, and then there was the great looking pub at the far end of the village. How could such good looking boozer go unnoticed by me for years?

It was only when we were about a mile or so from Southerness it occurred to me that I had once again failed to check up to see if the village's pubs would be open during our stay. Rural pubs quite often restrict their opening hours at certain times of the year. Although it was just after the Easter holiday I wasn't sure the main season began before June. If that were the case there was a real danger that John could suffer some sort of breakdown. If he was denied alcohol for an extended period there was no telling what would happen.

My concerns were not eased when, after getting off the bus, I looked over at '*The 19th Hole*'. There were no lights on and no movement in or around the building. The nearer we got to the hotel the less optimistic I became. Once again there was no sign of life. It was only when John, rather frantically, rattled the front door that we could breathe a sigh of relief. The doors opened and we could see a couple of people sitting at the top end of the bar.

Jordana, William and Louie in The Paul Jones Hotel

The interior of the bar had changed a great deal since my last visit. In fact the bar itself had been moved from the centre of the room over to the far wall. Back then it had the look of an old village inn. One side of the bar was mainly an area for the pint drinking man, while round the corner from there was the quieter part of the pub, and up a few steps at the back was the pool table. All that has now changed and the pub looks quite upmarket.

Of course the other great change from those bygone days was the lack of choking cigarette smoke. Everything in the place is shiny and clean. On my last visit even the barman had a ciggy permanently hanging out of his mouth and fag ash was often an ingredient of my pint.

We were still congratulating ourselves on finding such a great place to sit back and relax in when the barmaid dropped a bit of a bombshell on us.

Jordana Graeme had been listening to us talking about settling down for a bit of a session and thought she had better set us straight. The hotel bar actually closes at 2.30pm which gave us just enough time for one more really quick drink.

To say we were stunned by the news that the bar would be shutting in a matter of minutes would be a bit of an understatement. It has been a while since John has been rendered speechless but, for a few seconds, all he could do was make small whimpering noises.

Just when I thought we had made a huge mistake by coming to Southerness Jordana told us that the bar in the *19th Hole* opened as soon as *The Paul Jones* closed. I thought John was going to cry.

John, displaying his usual tact, asked Jordana if she ever got any stick from her customers over her unusual name. Fortunately she is used to dealing with daft old geezers and just laughed. In fact she went on to tell us that most people called her Pebbles.

Obviously we thought that was some sort of reference to the beach but a few moments later we found out that this was not the case. The hotel and *The 19th Hole* are both owned by Jordana's mother, who, we discovered, was sitting at the top end of the bar. It turns out that her name is Wilma and even John managed to work out the Flintstones connection: Wilma and Pebbles. In fact he was so pleased with himself we were treated to a five minute Flintstones inspired comedy routine, although I'm pretty sure he was the only person in the bar who thought it was even remotely funny.

It was bad enough Wilma and Pebbles had to listen to his nonsense but they had been joined by family friend Louie Robson. Unfortunately John kept referring to him as Fred. The poor man must have wondered what he had walked into.

I'm just glad that it was still early on in our day as we have been told that we can get a bit noisy after a few refreshments.

Apart from being a very nice young lady and a good barmaid, Jordana is a Scottish International golfer. Living right beside a golf course would seem to have paid off.

Down on the beach we set about scanning a 30 yard section of sand. Almost immediately we got a hit. It was time to deploy my newest secret weapon: the Treasure Seeker pin pointer. It's a hand held metal detector which is pointed into the area where a signal has been gained, narrowing down the area to be searched.

The great thing about metal detecting is you never know what is just under the sand. In this case the object of interest turned out to be a compacted piece of a tin can; at least that's what any sensible person would call it. John on the other hand insisted that it was clearly the top of an artillery shell. I tried to point out that if it had been part of a shell it would it would be in much smaller pieces. He wasn't impressed by my logic. God knows what he will come up with if we ever do find anything of value.

We spent about an hour on the shore and found yet another piece of of useless tin to go with our earlier find. Had it not been for the restrictions on our travel schedule we could happily spent a lot longer there.

There is only one bus every two hours from Southerness to Dumfries so careful planning is essential. Besides we fancied a beer or two in *The 19th Hole.*

Armed with the knowledge that this pub would definitely be open we confidently marched up the road. Over the years I have been in this pub many, many times. I was therefore keen to see how much it had changed since the last of those visits.

It had hardly changed at all. There is a small lounge bar to one side of the building where, especially at the height of the season, those of us who prefer our refreshments out of sight and sound of screeching weans can relax. The main hall of the pub is where much of the resort's night time entertainment can be found. I was glad to see that the owners had kept the original pool table in the place. John's reaction to it was priceless!

It is a hexagonal table, the only one of its kind that I have ever seen. John was so busy doing a double take of it that he very nearly did himself a severe damage with the corner of a bar stool.

Liz Ball, behind the bar in The 19th Hole

There were only a few other customers in the place, so we had a chance to chat to the barmaid, Liz Ball. She has been working there for years and lives in a nearby caravan during the holiday season. Apparently there is entertainment on in *The 19th Hole* every night. And, of course, the *19th H*ole is conveniently placed to revive the spirits of the golfers from the course next door.

The great thing about being right at the end of the road is

that it is almost impossible to miss the bus. It has to come into the village to turn. Even John on one of his many off days would have to get really creative to bungle the travel arrangements.

When we got back to Dumfries we once again had some time to kill before we got our bus back up to Hamilton. John was not surprised when I announced that we had to give *the White Hart* one last go. I was determined to find out what it was like in there. Its name suggested that it would be all tartan wallpaper leather armchairs and horse brasses. I'm glad I didn't put a bet on that. What a let-down I suppose the more you look forward to something the more likely you are to be desperately disappointed when you get it.

I had been expecting traditional Scottish but what we got was downmarket Vegas. We had to nip back up to *The Douglas Arms* for a quick pint and a reality check before we made our way home.

John; ***A review of the day;*** The sun shone almost all day and we had a brilliant time in Southerness.

Our treasure hunting was a great success, that is after assembling all of Craig's gismos. An Ikea chest-of-drawers holds no fears for me now.

The two pieces of metal we found (see photographs) were interesting, especially the round piece, which to me looks like to top of a world war two shell. What do you think?

We finished our day with a couple in *The 19th Hole* before getting our wee 372 back into Dumfries. As we had an hour or so before our bus back to Hamilton, Craig insisted that we check out *The White Hart* again to see if it was open. Unfortunately it was. Inside was like a brothel, and the barmaid, or madam I think they're called, had taken our order before we could turn round and escape. We downed our drinks as quickly as possible, exited and made our way back up to *The Douglas Arms* for a bit of normality and a couple more drinks.

We slept most of the journey back to Hamilton, where we had no trouble getting a 201 back to EK. Another great day on the beach.

Today' s finds

John's thoughts on today's finds;

The find I thought was very interesting was the round cap-like piece of ancient metal. To me it looks like the cap of an un-fired shell. This could have come from a naval ship sunk with the shells on board still unfired. What do you think?

Craig's thoughts on today's finds;

It looked as if we had once again found two pieces of scrap metal. We might not be lucky but we do seem to be consistent.

How to get to Southerness Beach
(by Bus from Buchanan Street Station)

Stagecoach X74 (Glasgow to Dumfries via Hamilton-2 hrs.
No. 372 From Dumfries Bus Station (about 40 minutes)

Rothesay (Kerrycroy Beach)

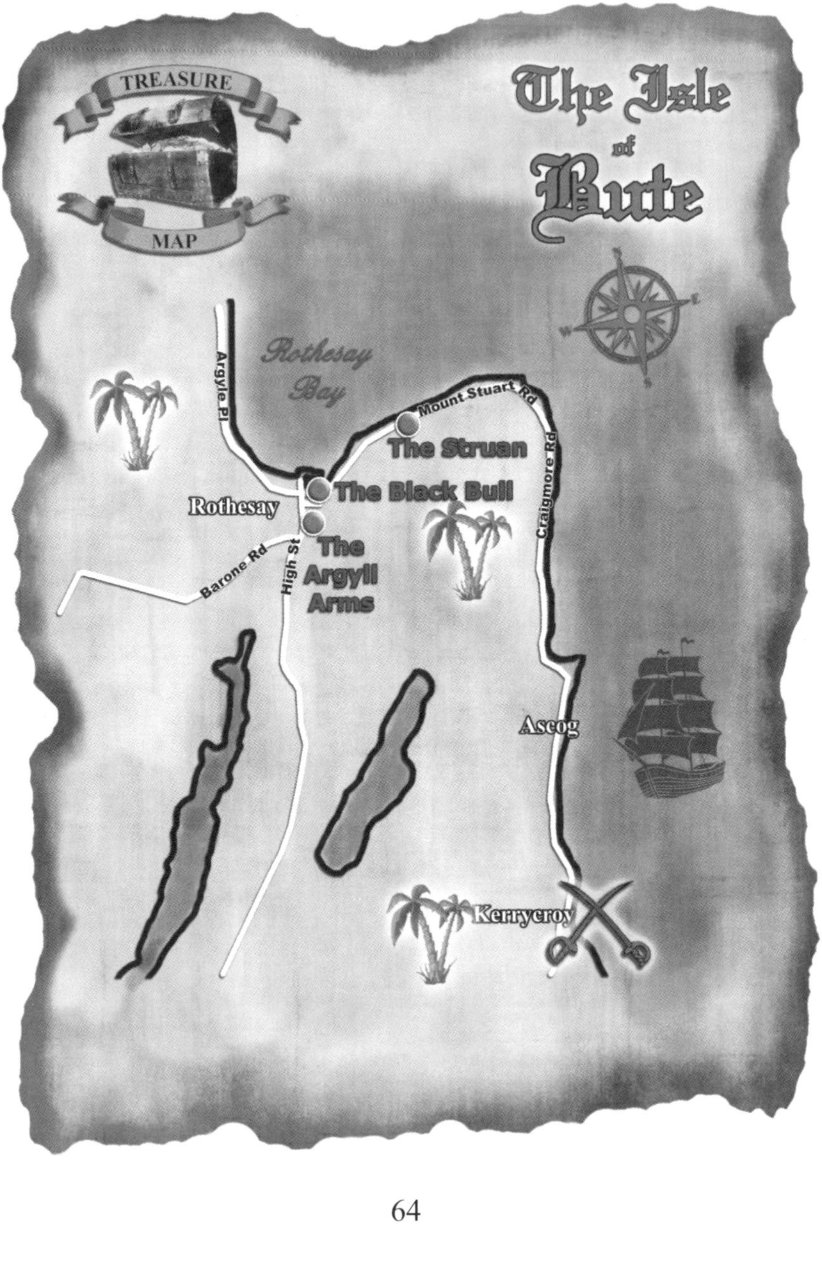

John; ***The Journey;*** Rothesay was my first suggestion for a place we should visit to find treasure hidden on beaches. As most of you may know, my Grandmother and Grandfather lived on the The Isle of Bute when I was young, and I cannot understand why I have not already found some treasure on it. After all, I must have spent years on the island's beaches when I was a boy.

As I am sure will happen a few times in this book, the question of how we are going to get to our various destinations, keeping to our religiously held convictions, to always go by bus for nothing, are going to be raised. Could there be a reason why sometimes we should take the train. 'Sacrilege'! I hear some of you cry. 'What happened to the bus pass?'.

We had a couple of options. By bus would mean almost an hour on the 18 into George Square, a 10 minute walk up to the bus station, then about 1 hour and 40 minutes on the McGills 'Clyde Coast Flyer' to Wemyss Bay. Alternatively, we could take the train. A half hour run into Central Station, then 50 minutes to Wemyss Bay. I explained to Craig that although it meant going against his faith (spending money), we would be saving over an hour each way. This means over two hours extra that could be spent searching for treasure, or, more likely, in the pub. Also, the idea of sitting for a couple of hours on a bumpy bus home after a good few pints didn't bear thinking about.

Craig pretended that it made sense to go by train. I'm sure he had no intention of ever going on the 'McGill's Flyer'. The seats must be the hardest of any bus in the country. Also, McGill's PR man must have some sense of humour calling 1 hour and 40 minutes from Glasgow to Wemyss Bay 'Flying'.

At about 9.30am I collected Craig and our equipment and got the 201 along to Hairmyres Station. As is my norm, I bought myself a black coffee in Glasgow Central for the journey, and as usual it was so hot we had passed Paisley Gilmour Street before I could drink it without scalding myself.

The sun was shining as we sailed into Rothesay Bay, which

must be one of the most beautiful settings in the whole world- honest.

A new good thing, apart from the bus pass, that the Scottish government have achieved, is to get McBraynes to reduce the fares on all Ferry journeys in Scotland. The fares are still not cheap, but they are quite a lot cheaper than before. Just like the bus pass, I'm sure the Scottish Government are subsidising it with our tax money. Yes, most pensioners still pay tax. So we are subsidising our own cheap travel. Our SNP editor Ian says I am talking rubbish!!

On the journey we had discussed which beach to visit. The two most well-known beaches on Bute are Ettrick Bay and Kilchattan Bay, but my favourite on the island is Kerrycroy, just before Mount Stuart House. It is a beautiful wee beach in an idyllic setting. It also fitted in well with bus times, so we agreed on it.

I had high hopes of finding treasure with a nautical background, which is my favourite kind.

Talking about the island and nautical things, an interesting fact that very few of you will know is that during the Second World War, the battleship HMS Hood was moored in Rothesay Bay when she got the message to head out to the Atlantic to search for, and destroy the German Battleship 'Bismark'. Unfortunately, we all know the tragic outcome of that encounter.

Even fewer of you will know of the true story of Craig's Irene and her association with the Hood. Irene had an uncle called James Riddle (honest, that was his name) who was one of the crew on the 'Hood'. Now when the order came for the 'Hood' to set sail right away, James had been transferred to the Isle of Crete to carry out some other task for the Navy, we don't know what! So he missed sailing with the 'Hood', and being killed in the Atlantic.

You can imagine his feelings of sadness, mixed with relief, when he heard about the sinking of the 'Hood'. A day or so later he was working at the harbour in Crete when he was knocked down and killed by a lorry! When it's your time, it's your time.

But back to today's trip. Naturally, before getting our bus from Guildford Square, which left at 1.45pm, we had to visit some pub to find out from the locals where the treasure was to be found. The fact that if the locals had any idea where treasure was they would have dug it up by now never enters our heads. We decided to visit *The Black Bull.* It's a pub we have never visited before on our previous trips to the island. It is also the pub that most of the yachting people drink in after a hard day's sailing, so it stands to reason they would know where treasure is to be found? In we went. As usual, I will let Craig fill you in with the rest of the day. I'll comment later.

Craig; *Today's Bars and Beaches;* John's favourite island, apart from Tenerife, is The Isle of Bute, and from the minute we decided to visit some of Scotland's most famous beaches he has been demanding that we include it on our schedule. To hear him talk you would think it was treasure island down there.

Since we had already visited one of my old holiday haunts I couldn't come up with a really good reason for turning down his request. So, like it or not, we were heading down the Clyde to check out the delights of Rothesay and its nearby beaches.

My only request was that we should visit some pubs we had never been in before. I've been in some of John's favourite pubs so often some of the bar staff think I'm a local.

With that in mind we headed straight for *The Black Bull* the minute we got off the ferry. To be honest my hopes were not exactly high when I first set eyes on the place. It looked suspiciously shut to me, but John assured me that it always looked that way.

The 'real' entrance to the pub was not at the front but at the rear, on West Princes Street. My first impression of the place was a bit run down and on the dim side. I soon changed my mind though. The bar in *The Black Bull* was atmospheric and friendly.

We were soon chatting to some of the other customers and

the barmaid. Morag Mackenzie has lived on the island since 1960 and works part-time in *The Bull*.

She told us that the bar gets really busy once the main season begins. Overlooking the harbour, or the Marina as some people insist on calling it, the pub is ideally situated to serve the drinking requirements of the yachting crowd who stop off in Rothesay.

Morag Mackenzie, behind the bar in The Black Bull

I have been told, by people who claim to know what they are talking about, that the West of Scotland has some of the best sailing in Britain. Apparently it has something to do with all of those little islands out there providing magnificent scenery and tricky navigation.

While I was chatting to Morag she pointed out a bloke at the end of the bar who, she said, had an unusual claim to fame. His name was Ian and according to Morag he collected seaweed.

I said that I couldn't really see the attraction of making a hobby out of collecting slimy vegetation. After all, once you've seen one bit of seaweed you've pretty much seen as much of the stuff as you will ever need to. But Ian set me right. He actually sells the seaweed to hotels and restaurants. He has also been featured in a couple of TV programmes. One of his most famous customers is the well-known TV chef, James Martin.

It turns out that John has known Ian for years and he knew all about his seaweed franchise and list of famous customers. This bit of news surprised me as John doesn't tend to keep things to himself, although I have often pleaded with him to do just that.

We were joined at the bar by a young couple, Iain Pollock and Nicky Headridge, who expressed an interest in our metal detecting scheme, or it could just be that they wanted find out if we were working some sort of scam. I'm pretty sure they didn't believe we intended writing a book about it.

Somehow John also caught this impression and quickly dug a few of our previous books out of the bag, just to show them that did in fact write books and were not just a couple of delusional drunks.

He was so successful at proving his point that Nicky bought both of the books. There may have been a hint of embarrassment involved in this transaction, but money is money. Instead of putting the cash away to bank later, we decided to put it towards a good cause: the kitty.

It somehow came out in conversation that Nicky worked for the council, specialising in hygiene within the licenced trade. John was very impressed when he heard this and instantly, and annoyingly, dubbed Nicky the Cludgie Inspector.

If anyone ever had their work cut out for them it was this young woman. I have to go into those places, due to the consumption of booze; a full bladder can be a powerful motivator. As the saying goes, when nature calls, sooner or later it has to be answered.

Visiting foul-smelling toilets for anything other than a medical emergency seems wrong to me, so you do have to admire Nicky's commitment.

Nicky Headridge and Iain Pollock

Eventually we got onto the priority subject of our visit, finding the best place to look for treasure. When we had been planning this outing John, who had been very keen to show what a really great choice The Isle of Bute would be, had mentioned no fewer than three different beaches.

Two of them, Kilchattan Bay and Ettrick Bay, turned out to be too difficult to be of use to us in the time we had to spend on the island.

The remaining beach, at Kerrycroy, seemed much more reasonable. Fortunately for us Morag agreed that we had made the right choice.

Kerrycroy was where a lot of the building materials and furnishings for Mount Stuart House were brought onto the island. With any luck some of that valuable stuff might have been lost in transit. Although what we would do if we found an 18th century marble column I'm not entirely sure.

Mount Stuart House is definitely worth a visit. It is the ancestral home of the Marquesses of Bute and has one of the best private collections of paintings and tapestries in the country. It even has its own marble-covered chapel.

Incidentally, the marble which covers the chapel from ceiling to floor was imported from Carrerra in Italy. That is the same quarry Michelangelo got most of his stock from, and as you can imagine it was not cheap.

Although it might sound as if I like Mount Stuart House, the fact is the whole place annoys me no end. All those wonderful paintings, fancy furniture and unbelievably expensive marble was paid for using the profits the family made off the backs of miners in Ayrshire and South Wales, two of the poorest areas in the country at that time.

If, by chance, we found anything of value on the beach at Kerrycroy I would take that as a bit of payback. The beach is conveniently close to the main road and therefore we were set up and ready to start scanning less than ten minutes after getting off the bus.

Almost immediately we got a signal on our detector. That actually became the pattern for the rest of the day. Every few minutes the machine would be bleeping like mad. Then, after digging a foot deep trench, the signal would disappear.

Legend has it that the Duke built his own stretch of railway from the pier to transport his ill-gotten goods up to Mount Stuart House. With all the ground signals we were getting I was a bit concerned that maybe he had buried his wee train set when he finished tarting up his house.

With only about ten minutes left before we were due to catch our bus back to Rothesay, one of our signals actually paid off. When I say paid off I mean in relative terms. To hear John tell it what we found was one of the original rail clips from the Duke's old railway line.

As far as I'm concerned we had spent more than an hour traipsing up and down Kerrycroy beach and all we had to show for our efforts was a large piece of bailing wire.

Metal detecting can be thirsty work and it is therefore a good idea to take a refreshing 'soft drink' along in your equipment bag. Fortunately it was such a cold day our soft drink cans didn't get a chance to overheat. It was while I was enjoying my refreshment that it occurred to me that the modern ring pull you find on cans these days has changed metal detecting. In the past those wee pull off rings littered every beach in Scotland, especially after the odd sunny day which tends to bring out the beach boozing masses. The debris they left behind would drive the poor wee metal detectorists daft.

Given all the rogue signals we had been getting on the beach, if someone hadn't invented the new ones we could have been there all day.

Since we were on John's home ground, so to speak, I decided to let him choose the next pub we could visit. I like to make him feel important and besides, the nearest pub was *The Struan.* Every time he goes to Rothesay he visits *The Struan* and bores me rigid with stories of what he got up to in there when he comes back. I was looking forward to checking it out for myself.

Unfortunately, John couldn't quite remember if there was a bus stop close to this pub, so he decided to chance his arm with the bus driver and drop hints about where we were going. To my great surprise this tactic worked and the driver let us off right outside the pub.

It was really a double surprise. On our extensive travels we have found that bus drivers in the West of Scotland tend to be a bit less than helpful when it comes to helping their passengers off at any point other than a designated bus stop, sometimes not even then. We reckoned that today's driver was probably just out of bus driving school. Obviously the other surprising thing was, John came up with an idea that actually worked.

The Struan is on the bottom floor of a three story terraced building on Mount Stuart Road and has a marvellous view across Rothesay Bay.

John McCathur, some other bloke and
William Wallace in The Struan

Once again we were not sure if the pub would be open in the afternoon but we needed to give it a try. Our luck was in and we ordered up a couple of cool drinks.

There was only one other customer in the bar and I'm pretty sure John knew him. Then again he seems to know everybody on the island; it's that sort of place.

Usually I am keen to chat to the people we meet when we are out and about but, for once I was distracted from my duty. The customer's name was William Wallace. But he goes by the name of Bill to avoid having to explain to dafties that he has no connection with the freedom fighter of the same name. Anyway, Bill had stopped off at *The Struan* for a quick pint while out walking his dog.

Jade is the biggest Dulux dug I have ever seen. She is also very well trained and friendly. Like many dogs I have encountered, once you give in and actually clap them, they become very difficult to get away from. Every time I stopped she would clout me with one of her huge paws. There was to be no ignoring her so I just gave up on talking to Bill and our barman John McCarthur.

John Cumming and Debra Crawford, The Argyll Arms (Glue Pot)

Before heading back to the pier to catch our ferry back to Wemyss Bay John insisted that we visit just one more pub. *The Argyll Arms*, or *the Glue Pot* as it is still called by some locals, is an old favourite of his and it just wouldn't do to pass up the chance of a visit.

We actually managed a couple of beers and a short chat to barmaid Debra Crawford and customer John Cummings. Personally I thought they did really well not to laugh us out of the place. It's all very well telling people that you are doing a bit of metal detecting when you are stone cold sober and can speak without slurring your words, but John was well beyond that. When he started telling them about a railway under the sand at Kerrycroy I decided that it was time for us to get a breath of sea air.

John; ***A review of the day;*** Another brilliant day of treasure hunting and drinking; does life get any better? Kerrycroy was, without doubt, the most exciting beach we have visited. Our machine never stopped beeping, and although most times we came up empty, we made an exciting find. Before I tell you what I am sure it is, I will give you the background on how I have come to my conclusion.

Kerrycroy Beach and the stone jetty at the end of it are the closest landing site to Mount Stuart House. The Stuarts built this Gothic Revival style over-the-top Mansion between 1879 and 1900. The money spent on the house is legendary. Two of the many amazing facts about the house are that it was the first house in Britain, or possibly the world, to have a heated indoor swimming pool, and secondly, it was the the first house in Scotland to have electricity. There is also a chapel that is completely covered in white marble. It's amazing.

If you have not visited it, you should. It is fabulous inside. Craig, on the other hand, hates it because of his Auchinleck background, enough said.

But back to the relic. The marble, most of which was Italian, had to be shipped in, so a railway track was built from the stone jetty at the end of the beach up to the house, about a mile or so away. It is obvious to me that this piece of rusted history is one of the clips that were used to attach the rails onto the sleepers. So what you see in the picture is a piece of real Scottish history, though I'm sure the Jacobite's would argue differently. Enough of this riveting history lesson and back to today.

Craig will have given you details of the pubs we visited. For me, the pubs were like old friends. I have been in them all many times in the past. The nice thing was that in each of the four pubs we visited, I met guys I knew some from years ago. The nice thing is that most of them were standing in the same spot in the bar that they have always stood at. Is this a nice thing, or is it a bit sad? I think it's nice that some things, like me, never change.

We had a lovely sail back to Wemyss Bay, where the train was waiting to get us back to the Central Station, then on to EK. Irene collected us, and so ended another day on the hunt. I'm sure you'll agree from the picture of our 'find', that what we have unearthed, or unsanded, is a piece of genuine 'Scottish History'

Today' s finds!

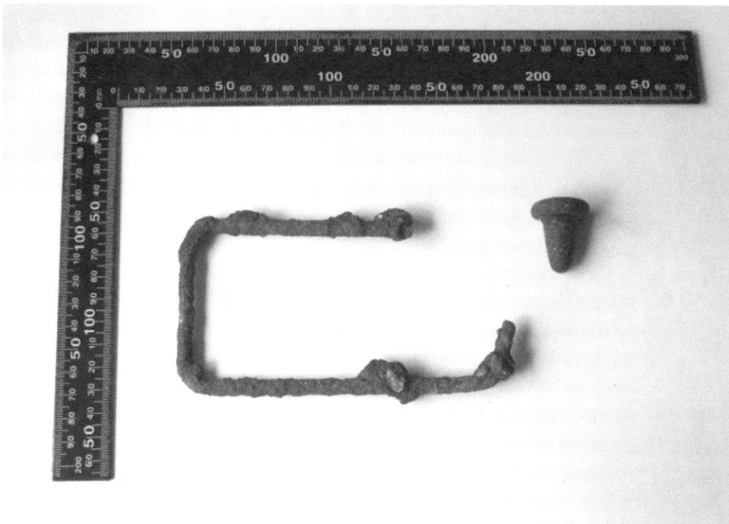

John's thoughts on todays finds;

As I mentioned earlier, there is no doubt in my mind that the photograph above depicts a clip used to attach the iron rails to the sleepers. I cannot think of any other explanation as to what it is, especially when you realise what went on years ago on that very beach.

The other small bottle stopper shaped item is obviously a stopper from one of the wine bottles used to refresh the sailors, probably a vintage Italian wine.

Craig's thoughts on today's finds;

I hate to admit it, but John might be right about the clip we found. It did look like the sort of thing that would be used on a railway line.

How to get to Kerrycroy Beach
(by Bus from Buchanan Street, also by Train from Central Station)

McGill's West Coast Flyer Nos. 901 or 906 Glasgow to Largs service will drop you at the Pierhead at Wemyss bay.
West Coast Coach No. 493 from Rothesay's Guilford Square will get you to Kerrycroy Beach in about 10 minutes.
If you are rich, go by train, from Central Station to Wemyss Bay.

Lamlash (on Arran)

John; ***The Journey:*** Lamlash, another of Craig's suggestions, but one I was in total agreement with. Considering all the Clyde-built ships, submarines and warships that have ploughed through the waters off Arran, it stands to reason that there must be ancient wartime and other things buried on the beach, just waiting for our *'Garrett Ace 150'* to discover roughly where they are, our wee battery operated pointer to tell us exactly they are, then our expandable trowel to dig them up. That, as always, was the plan.

Lamlash is one of these places that takes a hell of a long time to get to, especially when you plan to get there and back in a day, all on public transport. Now, as we traditionally use the bus, this makes the journey even longer than if we compromise Craig's moral high ground and go by train. I had to talk him into using the train. The idea of having to walk for 10-15 minutes down to the harbour did the trick. Craig's feet are his Achilles heel. I also offered to use the company card for the train and ferry tickets. His Ayrshire background couldn't resist.

Being a regular Cal Mac Ferry user on my journeys to Kate's sister Sheila in Rothesay, I had a timetable, which includes the train times to the Ferry Terminals, so was able to plan the journey in a few minutes. I even went on the web to make sure there were no delays due to sinkings etc. All was well. So at ten past ten I went down to Craig's house where Irene had the car ready to run us down to EK train station. An easy start to the day.

As usual, the half hour journey into Glasgow was less of a problem than the magic barriers at the end of the platform which always cause problems. My ticket would not move the gates no matter how often I tried. Eventually, a wee women opened the side gate and let a crowd of us through without even looking at our tickets. I've said it before, but British Rail would save money by removing the barriers and just having a couple of people collecting, or checking our tickets. There are at least two of them there anyway letting you through because the barriers are so temperamental.

If you agree that getting through the barriers is a nightmare, especially for people like me-daft-you should then go and try to buy a coffee in Costa Coffee. I wanted an Americano, which as far as I was aware was a black coffee, but you're not allowed to ask for a black coffee, and Craig wanted a Cappuccino. No idea how to spell whatever it is. The number of questions you are asked is amazing. What size do you want? are you sitting in? would you like our new, more expensive blend? do you want a carry case? do you want chocolate on the cappuccino? do you want milk in your Americano? By the time I got the coffees, I thought we might have missed our train. And another thing, if you put milk in a black coffee, it's a white coffee; jings, what a life.

Mind you, the wee carry case the girl gave me was magic for carrying the two coffees without burning your hands.

Our train was leaving from platform 13, which, as experienced train travellers will know, starts about halfway to the Clyde. I saw the barriers approaching, and was wondering how to get through them carrying the bag with our detecting material and pieces in one hand, and the coffees in the other, when the wee man kindly took pity on us and let us through the big gate at the side of the barriers without looking at our tickets.

The journey to Ardrossan Harbour passes through some well-known places, such as Johnstone, Dalry, Kilwinning, Stevenston, Saltcoats and Ardrossan. The great thing about going through these places by train is you only stop once in each town! Now I came from Govan and now live in EK, so I know what I'm talking about-one stop is enough!

A small piece of trivia you should know is that the stone wall along Ardrossan Town station is a thing of beauty. Next time you're passing through, it's on your left on the way to the harbour and well worth a look. I was so impressed, I asked Craig to take a photo of it for the book. He told me I was daft. I just told him that a thing of beauty like this is a local treasure, and should be in the book. It was then he admitted that he had forgotten to bring his camera. 'How the hell are we going to photograph our finds?' I asked. He claimed that his magic phone had a camera built in and that the lens was even better than his camera. By the time he had explained all this to me, we had left the station and 'The Wall' was gone. Hope we don't miss any other treasures today.

The Caledonian Isles was waiting for us as we left the train and walked down to the ticket office. It's a big ferry, and the inside was very luxurious, with lots of seating areas, some of which seemed very fancy, a nice snack bar for the non-alkies on board and a bar at the stern for Craig and me. So that's where we headed.

There was still about 15 minutes to sailing time and the shutters were still down on the bar, so I left Craig to sit and wait in case the bar opened early, and I had a walk round the ship. It was very nice.

Dead on sailing time, the shutters on the bar went up, and I raced over while Craig tried to hold back the other drinkers. It worked, I was first in the queue and we were soon enjoying our first pint of the day. By the way, it was 12.30 pm, so the sun was well over the yard arm, whatever that means.

A point of interest is that the distance from Ardrossan to Brodick is exactly 15 miles. The reason I know this is that I was asking Craig if he knew the distance when a wee Glasgow guy sitting with his wife at the next table shouted over, '15 miles'. I thanked him and told him that I wished my hearing was as good as his.

The sail over to Brodick lasted two pints and soon we were approaching the pier. Arran claims to be Scotland in miniature, and one of the most beautiful islands in Scotland, if not the world, and I would not disagree with that statement, but Brodick, and Lamlash for that matter, are nothing to look at. It's only a minor complaint.

As we waited to disembark (get off), there was a delay, then an announcement that the passenger ramp was not working and we would have to get off via the car deck ramp. Craig was raging as this would mean a long walk. As the other passengers raced away, Craig and I just stood for a moment until Craig worked up the energy to start walking. Lo and behold, if there was not another announcement telling us that they had found the 'on' button and the passenger ramp was now working. While the rest of the passengers had to turn round and make their way back up, Craig and I got off the ferry first. I was all chuffed. Craig could only mutter about what a shower of numpties the pier people were. There's no pleasing him sometimes.

Our local bus, the No. 323 (why such a big number) was waiting and whisked us to Lamlash in 10 minutes. It was a lovely journey, and the local golf course at Lamlash looks fantastic. Must make a point of visiting it in the future.

The bus dropped us off on the front, and the sun was shining as we walked along past an assortment of buildings which, in my opinion, did not fit in with the beautiful setting of the town. All of them were either too modern or ugly, and there was no symmetry to the layout of the place. However, we soon got to our first port of call, *The Drift Inn.* As usual, I'll let Craig take over from here.

`**Craig; *Today's Bars and Beaches:*** Our trip to Arran had been long in the planning but, as usual, we changed that plan at the very last moment. On the train down to Ardrossan I asked John how he felt about changing our destination from Brodick to Lamlash.

I really should have waited until we were sitting on the ferry with a drink in hand before bringing up the subject. He is always easier to persuade when there is alcohol on offer. As it was, I knew that I would have to come up with some really believable reasons for changing towns.

Over the years I have visited the island many times and have even stayed in four of Arran’s main towns. This I believe gives me a real insight into the quality of the facilities available to us in those places.

To cut a long story short I told John that the pubs in Brodick were all crap. The two pubs he had suggested visiting before and after our stint on the beach with the detector did not meet our high standards.

The Brodick Bar was the nearest pub to the beach, and I had been in it a few years back. In my humble opinion this pub was more like a wine bar than a traditional boozer. If the bar had been a bit busier I would have slipped back out without buying anything. Unfortunately there were only a couple of customers in there and they both turned to see who had just come through the door.

They probably couldn't believe that another unfortunate had fallen into the trap of thinking that *The Brodick Bar* was a real pub. After parting with an eye-watering amount of money I knocked back my pint of gassy brown liquid and got out of there as fast as possible.

I was pretty sure that I had made my point, but just to make certain I reminded John that the other pub he had planned on visiting, *Mac's Bar,* was at the other end of the scale.

We had 'enjoyed' a few beers in that place the last time we had been on a visit to Arran. The bar was manky, the beer was flat and the clientele was on the decidedly dodgy side. The way I remember it the service wasn't up to much either. If the barman could have thrown our beer at us he would have.

I could tell by the look on John's face that I had won my argument: we would be heading to Lamlash to hunt for treasure and beers. I suppose if I had just told him the truth - that I didn't fancy the walk from the pier to the beach and back again - he would have agreed with me. But where's the fun in that?

Our plan of action for Lamlash was to visit *The Drift Inn* for a couple of drinks and ask about the best area of the beach to try with our detector. After searching the beach we would then adjourn to *The Pier Head Tavern* for refreshments and an evaluation of any 'findings'.

Of course we got off the bus at the wrong stop and found ourselves standing directly across the road from *The Pier Head Tavern*: known to locals as the PHT. We were tempted to change the plan once again and stroll over to the PHT, but good sense prevailed and we made the slog back along the road to *The Drift Inn.*

It had been a few years since I had last visited *The Drift* but I did remember that it was not laid out like a traditional pub. It was more like a fairly large hall with a bar in it. During the day it had been a family friendly place and at night there was occasional entertainment.

The Drift Inn, Lamlash, Arran

As I say, that was a few years ago and I was sure that it would have changed quite a bit since then. However, I wasn't expecting the change to be so drastic. Instead of wandering into a wee beach-front bar it felt as if we had stumbled into the VIP lounge of an international airport. I half thought about wiping my feet before going up to the bar.

There were quite a few customers in the place, all of them sitting at tables having lunch. From our point of view things were looking grim.

Usually we like to see a nice clean bar, but this place was immaculate. John actually whispered to me that we could have eaten our dinner off the floor in this place, provided of course that we could afford to buy food in such an upmarket joint.

I caught a glimpse of the specials board and saw what he meant. As far as paying for lunch was concerned, a starter would have finished off our kitty.

On the bright side, it looked as if we might well be the youngest customers in the pub.

Things brightened up a fair bit when we started talking to the girls behind the bar. Hannah Murphy told us that *The Drift Inn* had at various times in the past been a house, a café and more recently a bar. To John's delight she also told us that the pub had its very own ghost.

He did stop laughing moments later when he discovered just how much the round had cost us. What he didn't know was that he was about to choke on his tongue when he got the bill for the next one.

John is forever going on about me always choosing to drink Tennent's Lager. He thinks it just a chemical mixture made to look like a lager. This, coming from a man who would drink paraffin if you put a wee touch of soda in it was a bit rich if you ask me.

Anyway, Hannah decided to give us both a wee sample of a craft lager which was proving popular with the locals. St Mungo's craft lager is brewed in Glasgow and I have to admit that it tasted very good. In fact I was so impressed with the sample that I ordered a pint of the stuff. Not to be outdone John ordered a pint of it as well.

We were savouring the brew when Hannah presented us with the bill. I reckon that John lost a good 50 pence worth of St

Mungo's finest when he found out that two pints of it cost £9.00.

There was a bit of a pause in the conversation while the bar and John were dried off with napkins.

We then asked the girls behind the bar where we might find the best areas of beach. Between them they came to the conclusion that we would be better moving up nearer the middle of the town to find good stretches of sand. Apparently the beach outside *The Drift* was a bit stony for metal detecting.

Hannah Murray, Lauryn Fleming and Ellen Sterns

I was quite happy to hear this as we intended finishing off our day in the PHT which is near the middle of the town. It was also the most traditional pub in the town and as such would suit us much better than another café bar type of place.

But when I said this to the girls they were less than enthusiastic. It would seem that the PHT had given up on tradition and had been turned into a wine bar. We were devastated.

Hannah suggested that we might have more luck if we tried *The Lamlash Bay Hotel*. She said it was the nearest thing to an old fashioned style pub that we were likely to find in the town.

A young bloke, who was sitting on a bar stool just up from me, joined in on our conversation. He said that the hotel wasn't bad, but he still preferred *The Drift.*

It turned out that this bloke was from Brodick and he quite often came over to Lamlash for a bit of a change of scenery. I asked him if he ever drank in *Mac's Bar* when he was out and about in Brodick, expecting him to say that he wouldn't be seen dead in there and describe what a terrible place it was.

He told us that the dreaded *Mac's* was no longer in business. I was shocked and had to ask if it had died of natural causes or had been forced to close.

He was under the impression that either the licensing board or the environmental health department had a hand in closing it down. Knowing what it was like in there I wouldn't be surprised if it had been declared a danger to public health and had its doors nailed shut. Hopefully with the bar staff still inside.

The young Brodick man then told us that he liked to have a beer or two in a pub called *Fiddlers*. I had never heard of the place and made a mental note to visit this new pub if we had time before we needed to catch our ferry back to Ardrossan.

Out on the beach we started scanning at a point just opposite *The Lamlash Bay Hotel.* That probably sounds as if we planned it but I can assure you that it was purely coincidental. It was the only point we could easily get onto the beach.

At first I thought we might have chosen the only stretch of beach on the island to be absolutely free of metal. The detector refused to make a sound as I swept it across the sand. It got to the stage where I had to test it by passing it over John's metal hip. The buzzer went off loudly, indicating that the machine was working properly and at the same time proving that John has his uses after all.

Eventually I did get a strong signal and John started digging around in the sand with his usual enthusiasm. Up until now that has meant spraying sand around to all points of the compass, but I had a plan to stop all of that.

One of the biggest problems we have when out on the beach is finding the metal objects again once they have been wheeched out of the sand by John's erratic shovel action. To concentrate our efforts I had bought a garden sieve. The idea was simple enough; I had to get John to load up the sieve with all of the sand he takes out of the hole, then, give the sieve a really good shoogle.

Not only would this help us find the objects faster, it had the added advantage of slowing the digger down a bit. But, as expected, he was less than complimentary about the new addition to the kit bag. In fact he scoffed at it. I could of course understand this reaction, as a plastic basin with lots of holes in the bottom of it might seem scarily high-tech to someone like John.

I could have predicted what our first find would be. So far, on almost every beach we have scanned the first thing we usually find is a piece of rusty wire; today turned out to be no different.

An hour or so after collecting that scrap iron we got a really strong signal from the detector. This time however the indicator on the machine was registering silver. I have to admit that seeing this got me a bit excited. When I told John about it he got a bit hyperactive with the shovel. The new sieve proved its worth when, after a good shake, we found a lump of silvery metal lying in the bottom of it.

Usually when we find something on the beach I just throw it into the bag to clean up later on. This time however, John insisted that I take a picture of this find and send a copy of it to him, just for his records you understand. He also, for some reason, became quite possessive about the equipment bag. It was like 'The Treasure of the Sierra Madre' all over again.

I blame myself really. While we were scanning the sand I had mentioned to John that I had done a bit of research on Lamlash. It seems that back in 1263 the Viking fleet, which went on to get a bit of a pasting at the Battle of Largs, might have assembled in the calm waters to be found between The Holy Isle and the settlement of Lamlash.

The Vikings, as we all know, were in the habit of making off with anything that took their fancy, so it is therefore quite possible that they would plunder any churches and farms in the area while they had a bit of time on their hands. I thought that there might be a chance that some of their loot could have been left on the beach.

As soon as the detector indicated that the lump of metal we had uncovered might be silver, I could guess what was going through John's mind: Viking plunder, and the need for drink.

Once we had checked every grain of sand in a three feet radius of where we had found the 'mother lode', we decided to pack up our gear and make our way over to *The Lamlash Bay Hotel* for a wee celebratory drink.

Before we could do this however we were approached by a lady who had been strolling along the beach. She had seen us working on the sand and had come over to ask if we had found anything interesting. She had just finished asking when I noticed John edge a little closer to the equipment bag. Obviously he was taking no chances with our treasure trove.

The daft thing was, we were about to come into even more riches on the beach. Isabel, the curious lady and potential silver bandit, was intrigued when she found out that we were writing a book about our treasure hunting adventures. And when she discovered that we had some of our earlier books with us she insisted on buying a copy of 'The Auldest Boozers in Toon'.

With the cash from that sale in hand we hurried across to the hotel to convert it into liquid refreshment. However, since this was Arran, the money from the sale of the book it took us a year to write didn't cover a single round of drinks.

The Hotel had been recommended to us because it had the most traditional bar in the town, but I would have to say that describing the interior of that bar as traditional was to misunderstand the meaning of the word traditional.

The bar was still very modern in style, with grey stone brick walls and mahogany shelves instead of a real gantry. On the customer side of the bar things were a bit more traditional. Thankfully there was no food being served and, unlike the other 'designer bars' in town, the customers in this pub were a bit more like us; i.e. getting on a bit and thirsty looking.

The Lamlash Bay Hotel, Arran

I didn't actually fancy our chances of getting our hands on a drink any time soon, as everyone seemed to be waiting to be served. But our barmaid, Kathryn Allan, made quick work of it. Once everyone had been served we got a chance to talk to her. She told us that the hotel bar had a good local clientele and also attracted its fair share of the tourist trade.

I was still complaining, perhaps a little loudly, about the pubs in Lamlash being a bit on the posh side for the ordinary West of Scotland punter on a day oot doon the watter when Kathryn dropped a bit of a bombshell.

Apparently, my all-time favourite pub in Arran, *The Blackwaterfoot Lodge*, had given up the ghost and been turned into a bistro. Even the big hotel in Blackwaterfoot, *The Kinloch*, has had its bar renovated. I had never been too keen on it but at least it had been a real bar.

Kathryn Allan

Apart from finding a potential fortune in silver and selling one of our books to a fan on the beach, my day out in Arran was turning into a bit of a nightmare.

The one hope I had left was the new Brodick pub I had been told about. Despite Lamlash and Brodick being only three miles apart travelling between the two towns is not very easy. The bus service is not exactly frequent, with only one bus per hour. To make it back to Brodick in time for our ferry we had to catch the next bus. This meant that we would have about an hour to kill before our sailing.

One of the customers in the hotel had told us where this new pub was. He didn't sound too keen on the place but I was determined to finish off our trip with a visit to a decent, good old fashioned boozer.

The wee chap who had first mentioned the pub in Brodick actually got on our bus. He was heading back to town to visit *Fiddlers* so we asked him to join our company. As soon as we walked through the door of the place I was wishing we had thrown the wee bugger off the bus.

We found ourselves standing in what can only be described as an upmarket café, which, as an afterthought, also sold beer.

By this time we were getting used to paying a small fortune for our drink so when the young Australian barman demanded enough cash to pay his wages John barely twitched.

Up at the bar we chatted to an American couple for a while and were actually quite enjoying the experience. Had we been on our own I very much doubt that we would have ordered another round, but as it turned out it didn't really matter what we wanted to do. We were refused service.

Generally this only happens when John goes off the rails a bit and starts rubbing people up the wrong way. This can take the form of inappropriate language and/or sharing his strange political viewpoints with people who wish he wouldn't. But for once he was totally innocent.

It seems that *Fiddlers* stop serving drinks to customers at about 6 o'clock, if they don't order a meal. We were shocked into silence. Apart from the fact that I wouldn't give these chancers one more penny, even if a gun was held to my head I don't think I could have afforded anything on the menu. I doubt very much if I could have pronounced most of the items on it anyway.

We said our goodbyes to our American friends, made a rude gesture at the Australian behind the bar, and stormed out of *Fiddlers*, never to return.

You would think that by this time we would have learned our lesson: you would be wrong. *The Douglas Hotel* had reopened a couple of years back and I remembered that at one time the bar in it had been quite good. I was hoping that they might have kept it the way it was.

They hadn't, it was a big soulless place with all the charm and character of a very luxurious waiting room. For some reason the staff were all dressed like air stewards and had obviously been instructed not to smile or chat to the customers.

By the time we finished our drinks I was actually reminiscing about the good old days in *Mac's Bar.*

Our day out in Arran was over and we were glad that we had made the effort to get there. Despite not being too chuffed with the type of pubs we visited in Lamlash, the service and friendliness of the bar staff went a long way to making it a good visit.

Brodick was unbelievable, in the sense that I can't believe we were daft enough to go there.

John; ***A review of the day;*** It was a lovely sunny and warm day as we we unpacked our bag with its ever-increasing amount of equipment. The latest gismo Craig has bought is a plastic griddle sort of thing which allows the sand to run through it, but any larger item is kept in it for further inspection. Although I nearly fell about laughing at it at first, it turned out to be a great help in sifting the sand.

After about 15 minutes of false alarms, we got a strong signal, and after about 10 minutes of digging and sifting, we found what I am sure is an ingot of Silver. It could be worth a fortune. Later we dug up a flange sort of thing. Craig said it was just rubbish and wanted to throw it away, but I insisted it was photographed and kept for further inspection. It could be from an old warship!

Although we had a great time on the beach, the pubs were a different story. During the last six books, we have visited over 500 pubs. The four we visited today were all more expensive than any of the first 500. Arran, in my opinion, is definitely a place for the well-off tourist.

Having said that, the staff in the pubs, or bistros, were, in the main, all right, especially in *The Drift Inn,* where the girls behind the bar were great fun, and good at their job. It takes a lot for Craig to leavc a pub happy, after spending £9.00 for two pints. As I said, the Island is a wee bit touristy.

With Craig vowing never to set foot again in this posh, touristy, working-man hating place, we caught the 7.20pm ferry for our sail back to Ardrossan.

I have one major complaint to make about the ferry. Every window on the ferry is about a foot too high. If you are not six feet six, and want to look out at anything other than the sky, you have to stand up. It seems crazy when Cal Mac have spent thousands putting in luxury seating in lovely viewing areas if all you can see is the sky. There must be a reason, and if I can be bothered I will contact Cal Mac and ask them.

The rest of the journey went by in the usual manner, i.e.we slept most of the way. All this beachcombing is very tiring. Irene was at EK station to collect us. I think she was surprised that we were relatively sober. Well, for us anyway.

Today' s finds

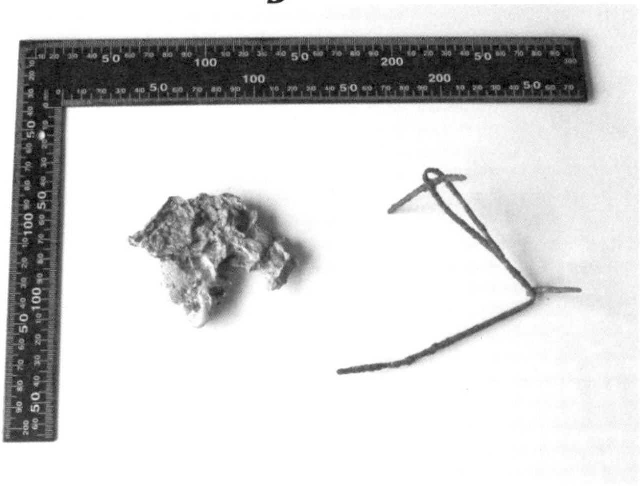

John's thoughts on today's finds;

The two finds today are possibly the most interesting to date. The Silver Ingot in particular could be worth a lot of money. Even the extremely old flangy looking thing could turn out to be from some old warship. Write in with your suggestions.

Craig's thoughts on today's finds;

It might actually be worth having the 'silver ingot' checked out. However, I'm fairly sure that John has no idea what a flange looks like or what purpose it serves.

How to get to Lamlash
(from Buchanan Street Bus Station)
(or from Glasgow Central Rail Station)

By Bus; X36 Glasgow to Ardrossan. Takes about one-and-a-half Hours. Get off opposite dock Road on Harbour road. It's a 10 minute walk from there down to the Cal Mac Terminal

At Ardrossan Harbour; Get on the big boat. You can't miss it.

At Brodick; At stance 4, get the 323 Blackwaterfoot Bus to Lamlash. It's only 10 minutes.

Irvine Beach

John; ***The Journey:*** Our decision to go to Irvine today was only made the night before. We were planning to go further afield, perhaps even the East Coast. But one of the thousands of gismos or Apps Craig owns told him that there was going to be stormy weather in the east.

This was the first day in May, so winter weather was to be expected! It was early in the book, so we still had plenty of alternative beaches to choose from, so we decided to go to the nearest one we had not yet visited; step forward Irvine.

I have been on the Irvine beach many times and on a nice day there's nowhere better. It's finding the nice day that's the problem. The best thing about the beach is that it's only a five minute walk to *The Ship,* one of the best, and oldest pubs in the country. And the food is fantastic. As usual, I'll let Craig give you the details.

At the end of the chapter I will tell you how to get to Irvine Beach from Glasgow, but we people blessed with living in EK go a shorter route. It is only about half an hour on the X16 to Kilmarnock, then the same again on the No. 11 along to Irvine high Street.

I know Irvine fairly well. Kate's family lived there for years, and her sister Margaret lives along the road in Kilwinning. Using this experience, I knew there was a bus that went down near the beach, and as Craig is bad with his feet at the moment, I checked out the the service that would save them from being exerted, well any more than they get looking for treasure and pubs. The No. 21 was one of a couple that looked as if it would fit the bill. Mind you, nothing is guaranteed in the *Traveline Scotland* website.

It was a fairly late start, so I had plenty of time to make up my corn beef with English mustard sandwiches. plain bread of course. Kate asked me if I fancied a Doughnut. I love them so I got the packet out of the cupboard. As I was about to open it I noticed that the label said ring doughnuts! This got me moaning to her about stupid modern things changing our traditions. A doughnut is ring shaped. If it's not, it's not a doughnut! She said nothing.

Pieces and ring doughnut safely packed away, I went down to pick up Craig and the 'gear'. Craig's Irene gave us a run down to the EK Bus Station to save Craig's feet. It saved mine as well.

Our X16 arrived on time at 11.01 am and fairly whisked us down to Kilmarnock Bus Station. Craig had a laugh at me checking all the stances for the No. 11. I told him it would be a double decker. 'Just like the one at the next stance with the big number 11 on the front', was his smartarse reply. He thought he was hilarious.

I wanted to go upstairs to see where we were going, but Craig's feet were louping. So it was downstairs for the half hour run to Irvine, without seeing much from our low down seats.

We got off the bus a stop too early in the High Street in Irvine, so we had to walk a good bit to get our next bus. Craig gave me laldy, but I told him that if we had been upstairs, we would have seen better where we were going and would have got off at the right stop. He said nothing. A bit like Kate earlier.

After asking a couple of locals, we found the right stop and waited in brilliant sunshine until our No. 21 came along and took us down to the harbour and dropped us off right outside *The Ship.* Craig will take over from here and fill you in with details of our day in Irvine.

Craig; *Today's Bars and Beaches;* Things didn't quite go according John's carefully mapped-out plan for today's little excursion. Unfortunately that is not at all unusual. We had originally planned to go to Arran but due circumstances beyond our control we had to settle for Irvine.

That actually suited me fine as I fancied an easier day. It didn't turn out to be all that easy. John seemed to be having an off-day recognising numbers, particularly the ones attached to the front of buses. That and getting off and on said buses at the correct stops, made our day a bit more complicated than it should have been.

John had once again produced a large file of timetables and route numbers which he insisted on showing me as we waited at the bus stop outside my house. Of course, he managed to drop them just as our bus approached. He insisted that a sudden, and presumably localised, gust of wind had caught them. I tried really hard not laugh but I just couldn't pass up the chance of getting in a bit of early mocking. Little did I suspect that I would have more opportunities to mock him later in the day.

The good thing about this trip was that we were already sure we had a definite venue for our pre-beach scanning session. We like to loosen up with a few drinks before we start a shift on the beach. It's like athletes limbering up before a big race.

Christopher and Jamie Murray

The Ship Inn had always been our main target for the day because it is by far the best known pub in Irvine. I had a vague recollection of visiting *The Ship* many years ago, but even if my memory could be relied on, which it can't, there would have been many changes in that twenty-odd year interval.

It was a pleasant surprise to find that there was still a fine old traditional bar just inside the front door. It is of course a fair bit more upmarket than our usual haunts, but we like to think we are adaptable, especially when there is the chance of a drink being involved.

John was delighted to find that there was a serious lack of carpets in the bar. *The Ship Inn* is owned by brothers Christopher and Jamie Murray and has been in their family for over 25 years.

When we mentioned to Christopher that we really liked the more traditional type of pub, he told us that up until quite recently music had not been allowed in there either.

Between them, Christopher and Jamie gave us a short history of *The Ship Inn.* The building which now houses the pub was built in 1567. Originally it was an ordinary private cottage but, from 1688 to 1707, it was used for collecting customs duty for the Royal Burgh. After that date it became the Customs House. Even though it wasn't licensed at that time sailors using the harbour were known to frequent the house for the odd jar of grog.

When a new Customs House was built further along the River Irvine, the new owner of the cottage applied for a licence to serve alcohol, only gaining that licence in 1754, after a four year struggle with the authorities. That makes the pub not only the oldest in Irvine but quite possibly the oldest in Ayrshire.

Like many public houses, particularly in Ayrshire, *The Ship Inn* has a connection with Scotland's national bard, Robert Burns.

In 1781 Burns was living in Irvine and through joining the Masons became friendly with John Hamilton, the son of the pub's owner. John was so impressed with his new friend's work that he became a subscriber to the breakthrough Kilmarnock edition of his poems.

Another character who frequented the pub was Captain

Richard Brown who is credited with encouraging Burns to send his poetry to a publisher. The rest, as they say, is history.

If you are a devotee of the Bard you could say that *The Ship Inn* deserves some of the credit in bringing his work to the world. Equally, if you're not that keen on his work, you now know where some of the blame lies.

Being one of Irvine's if not Ayrshire's most famous pubs can have its drawbacks. Christopher told us that on just one day last year 500 people turned up looking to have lunch or dinner. According to Jamie it was an example of a perfect storm. It was a bank holiday and for once the sun actually came out, meaning everyone headed for the beach. It was a bit of a struggle, but the staff of *The Ship* managed to feed the masses.

On another occasion the patrons of *The Ship* were enjoying a quiet Saturday night when the front door burst open and a van load of policeman charged into the bar. The big Sargeant demanded to know where the fight was.

Christopher said that all the customers and staff were too stunned to answer straight away and that seemed to annoy the policeman. Eventually the sergeant told him that they had received a call saying a major incident was taking place in the bar of *The Ship Inn*. The penny finally dropped with Christopher and he asked the policeman if he knew that there was another *Ship Inn* down in Ayr. After a moment of awkward silence, the police retreated from the bar and presumably hurried down to Ayr to see if there was anything left of that *Ship Inn.*

Being conscientious metal detectorists we had intended moving on after one pint, but the combination of good story telling and Jamie buying us another round meant we were a bit late hitting the beach.

I have never really thought of Irvine as a holiday destination. As one of Scotland's New Towns it has always been more associated with industry than entertainment. Therefore I was pleasantly surprised at the facilities we found at the entrance to the beach. Modern working toilets and an unvandalised picnic area were a welcome sight.

There were a number of people walking on the beach but, for once, no one seemed the slightest bit interested in two old geezers shuffling about ‘hoovering’ the sand.

We quickly got a signal and John set about shifting some sand. It doesn’t seem to matter how often we do this, we still get a bit excited when that alarm goes off.

As usual the excitement was quickly followed by disappointment; old rusty coat hangers have so little monetary value.

This was repeated several times before we made our first real find of the day. What it was exactly that we found I could not say, but John could! He ‘knew’ instantly that it was either a piece of jewellery or else it was a major component from a First World War submarine.

Just as I was about to hand over the detector to John I got another hit. I could see the look of frustration on his face; it really should have been his find. Now I’m not saying he wanted it to be a false alarm but he wasn’t exactly putting his back into the digging.

What made things worse was the fact that this particular find turned out to be the biggest one we’ve had so far. It was an iron bar about two feet long and an inch in diameter. John nearly gave himself a hernia lifting it out of the hole.

Straight away he announced that this solid lump of iron was quite obviously a piston rod from the same submarine as the earlier piece. If he is correct in his assumptions, god help us, I reckon that by the time we finish our metal detecting for the season he will have enough spare parts to build his very own submarine. Either that or enough scrap iron to subsidize a good night out in a Wetherspoon’s pub.

It was time to get off the beach and find another good Irvine pub. That turned out to be a bit harder than we had thought. *The Marina Inn* was supposed to be our next port of call and I was really looking forward to visiting it as it had John's personal recommendation. He had been in it before and said that it was a really good pub.

When I got my first look at it I was less impressed. It was shut. I think that it now just operates as a private hotel, a hotel with no bar.

In the past I have made the odd mistake when planning our trips and I have been made to suffer for those mistakes by John. Now that the boot was on the other foot I decided to take my revenge in a quieter, more sophisticated manner than his usual hissy fits. Suffice it to say there was a fair bit of head shaking and exaggerated sighing going on, as I know he hates that.

Further along Harbour Road I spotted a big red T for Tennent's sign on a building. This was like a weary sailor spotting a friendly shore, and we headed for it at top speed.

It wasn't quite what we were expecting. Instead of a cosy harbour-side inn, we had wandered into *Irvine Watersports Club*. But as John pointed out, they did sell beer, so we decided to give it a go.

It was like a miniature version of a Working Man's Club, just a wee bit better decorated. We did have to sign in and pay a pound each but even then the cost of a round was still below the average price. It occurred to John that the longer we stayed there the more cost effective our visit would be.

As we settled down to save ourselves a fortune John happened to mention that there was another pub just along the road.

Given his recent track record I was a bit suspicious but, since I am a natural born optimist, I decided to give him the benefit of the doubt. And there was a lot of doubt, but I really wanted to end our day out in a real pub rather than a big empty club.

By the time we reached the next pub we only had enough time for one drink before we needed to catch our bus back into

Irvine town centre for the onward journey home.

The Harbour Lights looks every bit the traditional river side pub, on the outside at least. I had been expecting to see a bit of nautical paraphernalia; fishing nets, creels and ships in bottles. It wasn't a bit like that. The pub is light and modern with a fine long bar and plenty of sitting room. I liked it.

Emily Lee at the Harbour Lights

Our barmaid, Emily Lee, told us that she had only been working in the pub for seven months. I took this to mean that she had recently moved to the town from South Yorkshire, as her accent was still quite pronounced. But she told me that she had lived in Irvine for twenty years; she just hadn't lost her accent

I had to tell her that I was genuinely impressed as I've known people who had spent a fortnight in New York and came back speaking like someone who had been brought up in the Bronx.

The Harbour Lights owners, Amanda and Derek, bought the place just over a year ago. They have been upgrading it ever since and Emily said that they wanted to make it a family-friendly pub. It seems that, between them, Amanda and Derek have seven children so even I could understand why they might have to allow kids into the pub. That being accepted I still find this concept quite chilling but decided not to let it spoil what was likely to be my last ever visit to the place.

It was time for us to go and we made our way outside. The bus we had to catch was the No21 and according to the timetable they don't run that frequently. Missing this bus was not an option as we had two other connections to make.

John was getting a bit agitated, which was understandable given his batting average for today's trip. Maybe that's why he was looking in the wrong direction when the No. 21 rolled past us. It stopped across the road and I had to more or less drag him backwards over to it.

He was so grateful that he couldn't express himself. I was just glad we had made it onto the bus, and of course I now had something else to hold over him.

We had enjoyed another great day out, found some major components from at least one U-boat, if you believe John, and met some very nice people.

John: A review of the day; I really enjoyed our day in Irvine. The pubs we visited were all good, especially *The Ship,* which should have been featured in our last book, 'The Auldest Boozers in Toon' (£8.99 in all good Waterstone's) as it is one of the oldest in the country.

But, surprisingly for me, the highlight of the day out was the finds we made on the beach with our '*Ace Garrett 150'*. I know Craig does not agree with me, but our main find is, in my opinion, a piston from an old steam driven ship. I'm not sure if it's from a merchant or naval ship, but if you study the photograph, I'm sure you will agree it is interesting. The only down side of the find was that it must have been about a stone in weight, and I had to carry it home.

It was worth it, because it is one of our most interesting finds. Mind you, I'm taking nothing away from the ancient nail, the 'C' shaped flange thing, or the shaped wires, which I'm sure you'll agree could all be from the engine room of an old vessel.

I'm starting to enjoy this metal detecting thing. Craig tells me not to call it treasure hunting, as he says it makes us sound like a couple of numpties. I think that boat has sailed!

I really enjoyed our day in Irvine. The only moment of panic on the homeward journey, which Craig has already mentioned, was as we left the *Harbour Lights Bar,* I somehow managed not to see the No. 21 waiting on the other side of the road from the bus stop I was standing at. We got it after my version of a sprint across the road, which nearly caused a pile-up, as I also failed to notice a car approaching. Craig took the brunt of the car driver's road-rage as he limped across.

The rest of the journey home, including a quick one in Kilmarnock, went without incident, and we live to tell the tale.

Today' s finds;

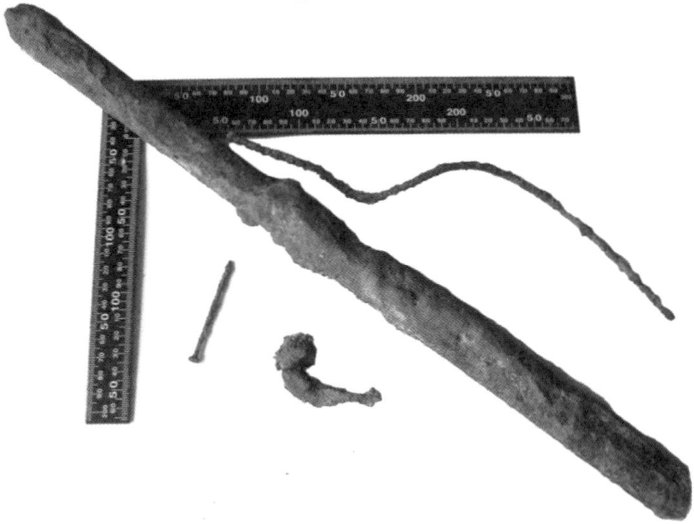

John's thoughts on today's finds;

Today's main find was one of the most exciting so far. As you can see in the photographs above, all the interesting items seem to be working parts from some engine room, but the large metal shaft is definitely from the piston of some old ship.

Craig's thoughts on today's finds;

If we were to sell the scrap metal we find on the beach by weight we could be rich soon.

How to get to Irvine Beach
(from Buchanan Street Bus Station)

The X34 or the X76 are two of the services that will take you straight to Irvine. Takes just over an hour.
From EK we get the X16 to Kilmarnock then the No. 11 along to Irvine.
The No. 21 takes you down to the beach from the High Street. If feet ok, it's a 15 minute walk.

Sandhead (Luce Bay)

John; The journey: and what a hell of a journey it is. I asked Craig why he wanted to go to such a far flung place. 'It's because it is so far flung that we must go', was his reply. 'We must show our readers that we have covered the four corners of Scotland'. I had no eloquent answer to such Auchinleck logic, so it was to the very South West corner we were off.

It was around the 10th of May, and it was one of the very few times in the year where the weather forcast was almost guaranteeing us a glorious day, and so it turned out. It was hard to have the nerve to put on summer gear for a whole day away, but I chanced it. No shorts, mind you.

Booking the bus both ways is essential, as it is usually very busy with people getting off at Cairnryan to catch the ferry to Belfast.

Kate asked me if I was going to take a salad instead of my normal corned beef pieces. 'It may be going to be a warm day, but the sun's no' gone to my heid yet', was my witty reply, (well I thought so anyway). So with no help from Kate, I was up at six in the morning to make my pieces, get ready and out to collect Craig at seven.

We got into Glasgow with no probems, and we had time to visit the local Sainsbury's wee store beside the Bus Station for a wee snack for the journey to Stranraer; it is two and a half hours after all! We were at our place at stance 54 in plenty time to get on the bus, which was surprisingly empty. I doubt if it was more than half full.

We left Glasgow at 8.30am in lovely sunshine and settled back to enjoy the journey south. By luck, good or bad I'm not so sure, two men, one in particular with an amazingly loud voice, sat behind us. It was ok for Craig, who had brought earphones with music playing through them. I was agog when he showed me the gizmo that the music was playing from. It was about the size of a Penny Caramel.

These two guys, who were both rampant Rangers supporters, were on their way to Belfast for a Monday to Friday holiday, and the one with the loud voice spent the journey shouting information about the places we were passing at his mate. Most of what he was saying was nonsense. Examples I can remember include: 'that's Turnberry Golf course, where the Open is being played this summer'; 'Cairnryan is the port we'll land at in Ireland'; ' We'll get a better tan if we go into the salt water first'; and my favourite one was when he spotted a P. & O. Ferry sailing out of Loch Ryan as we were approaching Cairnryan. 'That's the ferry to Liverpool, it takes six or seven hours'. His confidence in what he was shouting was staggering. It fairly shortened the journey for me. Mind you, so did the sleep I had in the middle of it. We nodded our farewell to the two guys, who were going to 'get a couple of pints into them right away to start the holiday'. To be honest, they sound a bit like Craig and me.

When everyone got off the bus at Cairnryan Terminal, we were the only ones left for the short run down into Stranraer. Before pulling away from the stop, the driver looked out of his window, then asked us if we had a bag in the luggage hold. 'We have that' Craig replied. 'Well I better put it back on the bus,' was his reply. He had thought everyone was getting off and our grip was lying on the ground. If we had lost the *Barrett Ace 150,* I think Craig would have killed the driver. All was well though, and at 11.05am, we said our farewell to the driver and stepped out into Stranraer in brilliant sunshine.

The sun helps to make everywhere look nicer, and it was doing its best in Stranraer, which, to be fair, is no mean feat. But I think it worked, the place looked smashing. As we walked along George Street, hundreds of locals were sitting outside cafes and other wee shops, and not just to smoke. It was warm! And everyone seemed to be smiling. The sun is magic! A word of advice to the over 30s. Nobody should be wearing shorts, especially before lunch.

The reason we were wandering along George Street was that we had about an hour and a half before our bus to Sandhead, so we were heading for a pub we had visited before and had a great time in. I think I ended up dancing on the tables. I'm sure Craig will fill you in with his version of today's visit.

At about 12.30pm, we got on the No. 407 for the 20 minute run down to Sandhead. Before starting our Metal Detecting (I'm not allowed to call it Treasure Hunting) we went into a small pub across the road called the *Tigh na Mara* for a talk to the locals and get a quick couple of pints right into us. Where had I heard that statement already this morning?

Craig; *Today's Bars and Beaches;* John was a bit surprised when I first said that I would like to visit the beach at Sandhead for our next expedition. He got a bit rattled about it and at first I thought that maybe he had spent a bad holiday there once or else owed someone from Sandhead money. But it soon dawned on me why he was so against going there; he had no idea where it was. Actually his mood didn't improve when I told him where it was. Going down there meant an awful lot of bus travel, probably about eight hours in total not counting the inevitable hanging around at bus stops waiting for buses which don't always run to timetable.

However, when I told him that there was a pub right next to the beach he calmed down and eventually agreed give Sandhead a go.

Obviously there is no direct bus service from Glasgow to Sandhead; a change over at Stranraer is required. Not only that but because there is only a limited bus service to Sandhead we found ourselves with an hour and a half to kill in Stranraer before we caught the bus to Sandhead.

We have been to Stranraer several times in the past and to be honest we have discovered that some of the pubs in or around the town centre belong on the 'to be avoided' list.

Fortunately we did know a good boozer and we headed straight for it as soon as the bus wheels stopped going round. **The** *Golden Cross* on George Street is a good old-fashioned pub and suited us down to the ground. The one worry we had was sometimes, if you leave it too long between visits, pubs change hands, staff leave or in a worst case scenario even the best pubs can go out of business. As soon as we clapped eyes on the pub we realised that none of these factors were in play. We could see Julie, the owner, standing outside the pub. But at first we didn't think she had recognised us, but after a bit of light-hearted swearing at us we realised that nothing had changed, it was just like the good old days. Eventually the conversation got round to what we were up to on the new book front.

Julie, Bradley and Kelly

When I mentioned metal detecting on the beach Julie looked at me as if I was a madman. If I cut down on the extravagant adjectives and the odd swearword, what she actually said was, we would be right out of luck searching for treasure in

Stranraer. But when I said we were actually heading for Sandhead she told us that we stood a much better chance there. Being a local I asked her if the bus we were supposed to be getting went beyond Sandhead, perhaps even on down to Maryport

At the very mention of that name Julie got even more verbally animated, if that were possible. It seems there was a bit of an incident the last time she was down near the bottom of the Mull of Galloway. She was representing her pub at dominoes against their rivals down in Maryport. The weather that night was terrible, rain and gale force winds causing havoc. The way Julie put it, if her team hadn't won the game maybe one of the opposition might have told them about the road conditions. As it was her car was caught in a landslide. Rocks, water and mud hit her car and caused extensive damage. They had to abandon it then try to escape the weather on foot. Her description of the conditions would make your eyes water, her description of the state of her clothing, including underwear, was equally graphic. We had to have another drink to calm her nerves.

Audrey and Tex, sadly missed

The laughs were coming thick and fast but Julie had a sad story to tell us. A nice old couple we had met on our last visit had died.

Tex and Audrey had been inseparable and on the day we met them we chatted to them for some time. Tex was a football man through and through. He told me many stories of his days as a player with Rangers. It seems that Audrey passed away first. After that Tex lost much of his cheery friendly character, sitting for hours just looking out of the pub window. There was shock but not much surprise when Tex passed away just a few months later.

Julie says the pub has never been the same since this nice old couple died. I suppose in pubs like *The Golden Cross*, when old regulars die, it's a bit like losing a member of your family.

We arrived at the bus stop to catch the 407 to Sandhead with plenty of time to spare. This surprised me, as we have a bit of a history in missing buses once we get to Stranraer.

I'm not really sure how many bus stops are in Sandhead, but, given the size of the place, my best guess would be one. That's why I couldn't understand why John was getting so worked up about up about getting off at the right spot. Of course there is a possibility that the three drinks he had downed in *The Golden Cross* had begun to work their way through his system and were demanding to be released. The man has a bladder the size of a gnat's.

Whatever the reason he was up standing next to the driver just to make sure the bloke knew that passengers were wanting off his bus. The stop is conveniently placed just across the road from *The Tigh Na Mara Hotel*, our main objective of the day.

Obviously, having never seen the place, I didn't know quite what to expect inside. But I was very happy to find a nice fairly traditional country inn. It has a low ceiling with original wooden beams, a nice long bar with stools and a good selection of draught beers. In other words, it was just perfect. From the bar you could look through to a lounge area and beyond into a beer garden.

Although the bar wasn't busy, the barmaid never seemed to stop. Apparently there is also a restaurant in the hotel and she was probably serving in there as well. Whatever it was that was keeping her busy, she didn't have time to stand and chat to us. Or maybe she had heard of us and wisely decided to keep her distance

We did talk to one local bloke, Bob Dunn, who lived just a few hundred yards away. After telling him what we were up to, he surprised us by telling a story about Scotland's role in a top-secret wartime operation. It seems that, for a time 617 squadron trained in the area, which until recently was still being used for live-fire exercises by the Air Force

Anyone who has had to watch television over any given Bank Holiday will remember that 617 squadron was also known as the Dam Busters.

Andy, Faisal the dog and Bob

Bob said that the bouncing bomb, developed by Barnes Wallis, was tested out in Luce Bay. The idea behind that was, Luce Bay has an extensive area of shallows and when the tide goes out it does so for a great distance. This allowed the technicians to walk out to inspect what was left of the bombs after they had been dropped. I have seen films of some of these tests and initially things didn't go too well. Until they got the height and speed correct many of the trial bombs shattered when they hit the surface of the water.

It is said that some of the early dummy bombs were encased in wood and were therefore especially prone to breaking up. That bit of news got John really excited. He obviously thought that there were bomb fragments out there to be found.

Of course, since he is totally obsessed by them, he had to ask about any submarine activity out in the bay. Bob gave him a look which I interpreted as ‘are you mad or what?, before explaining to John that there is barely enough water out there to float a boat never mind hide a submarine.

We were joined by another customer, Andy Mckay, who said that he had found coins in the sand up by the caravan park. Now it was my turn to get excited. I was thinking about Celtic gold or maybe a wee bit of Viking horde, but Andy burst that particular bubble when he told me that the coins he had found were in fact two pound coins, dated no further back than 2010. Rather than the coins being buried by a Viking raider it was far more likely that they had fallen out of the pocket of some poor drunk who managed to fall down a sand dune.

We finished our drinks, said cheerio to our new found pals and headed out to the beach to see what was to be found. The first thing I found was that sand was at a bit of a premium. The beach was stony with only small patches of sand. I was not happy.

I felt cheated, telling John that I had a good mind to report the whole town of Sandhead to the Trading Standards folk for pretending to have beach when all they had was a stretch of stony ground.

If you really want to check out the beach at Sandhead I suggest you invest in a pair of powerful binoculars and aim them up the coast at the caravan park.

John tried to calm me down by pointing to the small patches of sand and saying that there was enough there for us to scan. I really think that he was just trying to stop me from launching the equipment bag, containing his beloved *Garrett Ace150*, into Luce Bay. He has become very attached to that metal detector, which is surprising since he called it all sort of not very nice names when I first came up with the idea.

Despite the lack of sand we got a hit almost as soon as we started scanning. I was a wee bit disappointed when we dug up a rusty nail. But John saw it differently. This rusty four inch nail had historical significance according to him. It had obviously come from the casing of a Barnes Wallace bouncing bomb.

We must be really good at this history lark because we found a few more 'Barnes nails' in the next few minutes. The biggest problem so far as I was concerned was the lack of actual sand on the beach. John on the other hand thought that having a limited search area just concentrated our efforts. Personally, I think he just wanted to get things over with and get back to the hotel. What he didn't know was I was thinking the same thing.

Walking on this beach was like walking on cobblestones. I was just glad when it was time to leave the alleged beach and return to a comfortable bar stool in *The Tigh Na Mara.*

Instead, John decided that we should check out the beer garden and enjoy what he liked to call 'an alfresco swally'. I finished my drink as quickly as possible because, by that time I had had enough of the great outdoors.

Back in the bar we met up with David and Margaret, formally from Newcastle but now living in Sandhead. When David heard us talking about finding fragments of metal which may or may not have come from a bouncing bomb, he told us that he had seen parts of the targets the bombers used in the tests.

Apparently they can still be found in the sand just north of the caravan park. That was enough proof for John that what we had found was the real thing. I wouldn't be surprised if he tries to have our rusty metal appraised on Antiques Road Show.

I decided to change the subject and asked Margaret what had brought them to Sandhead to live. She told us that they enjoyed the largely unspoilt nature of the area. David thinks that tourists coming up from England rarely turn left after crossing the border. This denies the local tourist industry a lot of revenue but keeps the place nice and peaceful.

Margaret and David in The Tigh Na Mara

After a few more pints and a lot more banter, we had to leave to catch our bus back to Stranraer. It is really just as well that the bus service is so infrequent or we could have spent far too long in *The Tigh Na Mara*.

Because of the mismatch in our timetable we once again had some spare time in Stranraer. We are not known for our creativity, so we did what we always do and tried to find a pub close to our bus stop. Earlier in the day we had seen this big fancy pub, all frosted glass and pastel colours, and decided that we would rather sign the pledge than be seen drinking in there.

Unfortunately, it looked like that pub was the only one available to us when we arrived back in town. Just before our principles were put to the test John spied *The Stranraer Supporters Club* just up the road. This place was much more suitable for gentlemen of a certain age who prefer a pub atmosphere to that of a Club 18-30 disco. That being said the supporters club is still quite modern, but in a way that we can both handle easily.

Colin Herron, Stranraer Supporters Club

Our barman, Colin Herron, immediately spotted that we were not your typical *Stranraer FC* supporters and set about changing that situation. We were treated to a concise history of the football club with particular emphasis on their most recent games.

When the banter turns to football I tend to mentally turn off, but John was in his element. He knew some of the former players and at least one manager, so he was able to hold his own in the conversation.

He must have been saying the right things as Colin disappeared from behind the bar for a minute, returning with a present in the form of a football programme from 1980s. It was from the game against Celtic. We were both impressed when he presented it to us. Of course it might just have been part of his strategy to turn us into Stranraer supporters.

I think it was just as well we had a bus to catch as there was a serious danger of a drinking session developing. All that was left to do was to get on the bus, finish off the food we had left and fall asleep. We managed all three in a matter of minutes.

John; A review of the day: We had a great time in the three pubs we visited today, and Craig got some brilliant information about the potential for fabulous finds under the local beaches, including the one we were visiting today.

Although the tide was fully in (high), I was not as despondent as Craig about what was left of the beach to detect on. There were still bits of sand about and we set about them with a vigour brought about by the brilliant sunshine and a couple of drinks in us.

The finds we made today were amazing. If you study today's treasure photograph, like me, I'm sure you'll have no doubt that the thin piece of what looks like an 80+ year old steel is part of the inner casing of a bouncing bomb. The piece of steel about three inches long must be part of a shell of sorts, and the ancient nails speak for themselves. I mentioned to Bob, one of the locals in the pub across the road from the beach that our find might, in fact, be from a submarine, but he pointed out that the Solway Firth in the Luce Bay area is very shallow, and there are no records of midget submarines being tested in this area during the war, so they must be from the bouncing bombs.

Treasure hunting on our beaches is leading me to believe that there must be enough pieces of old ships lying under the sands to build a brand new ship, or submarine.

We finished our hunting, packed up the very heavy bag and wandered back over to the *Tigh Na Mara* for a wee drink in the beer garden, then another couple in the bar before heading out to pick up our 407 for the 20 minute run back into Stranraer. It was about 45 minutes before our coach back to Glasgow, so we passed the time very pleasantly in *Stranraer Supporters Club* where Colin, the barman, and supporter for over 50 years, gave Craig some great local information from the war years. He also gave us a copy of the match programme for the game about 40 years ago when Stranraer gave Celtic a run for their money in a cup match. It was much appreciated, Colin.

We were the only passengers for the 10 minute run out of Stranraer up to Cairnryan, and when we told our driver Gareth what we had been doing all day (apart from the drinking), he gave Craig some very interesting information about the area we were passing, especially during the war years, and just after.

Craig was a nightmare on the journey home. First of all he said that we would be able to get off the bus at the end of Bothwell Street, just before Hope Street. This would allow us to walk across Hope Street into the Central Station, saving him the 10 minute (or more in Craig's case) walk down from the Bus Station. The driver said the bus did not stop before the station. Craig was non too happy with this, but did cheer up a bit when I told him that we could get the wee circular bus that ran between Central, Queen Street and Buchanan Street. We got to the stop to find that the last bus of the day had left half an hour ago.

In a desperate attempt to save Craig's feet, and temper, I came up with the great idea that all the buses run straight down Renfield Street to Central Station, so he would not have to walk. Sure enough, after two minutes a No. 17 turned up and we jumped on. My relief, and Craig's I'm sure, turned to terror when the bus turned into Bath Street. It was on its way to the Clyde Tunnel! Would you believe it? I talked the kind driver into letting us off just after Hope Street on Bath Street and tried to convince Craig that the walk to the Central would not be any longer. I don't think he even answered.

We eventually got to the station. I mentioned to Craig that

we were getting the same train as we would have got even if we had got off on Bothwell Street. It didn't help.

Craig's feet settled down on the way back to EK. Mind you, we had to sit facing backwards. Craig hates sitting this way. God knows why. Irene was waiting to run us home and bring to an end a fantastic day in Scotland's most South Westerly point.

Today' s find' s

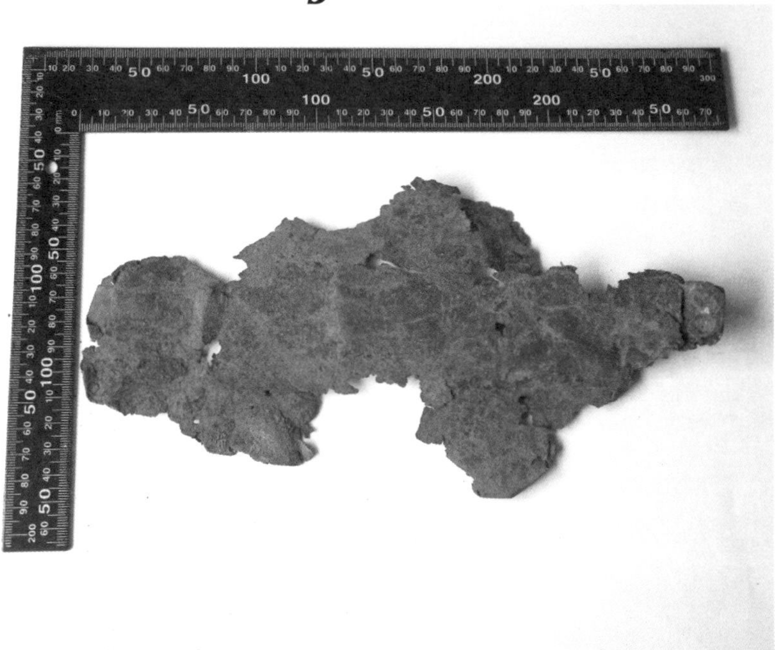

John's thoughts on today's finds;

When you study the photograph above, I think you must agree that the piece of interestingly shape metal fits the desctiption and overall shape of the Bouncing Bombs, which (and this is no coincidence) were tested on this very stretch of coastline.

Craig’s thoughts on today's finds;

More rusty metal for me to lug home.

How to get to Sandhead
(by bus from Buchanan Street Bus Station)

No. 923 Citylink/Ulster Bus will get you there in about two and a half hours. Make sure you book.
No. 407 Will take you to Sandhead in about 20 minutes. Check times as not too regular.

Girvan

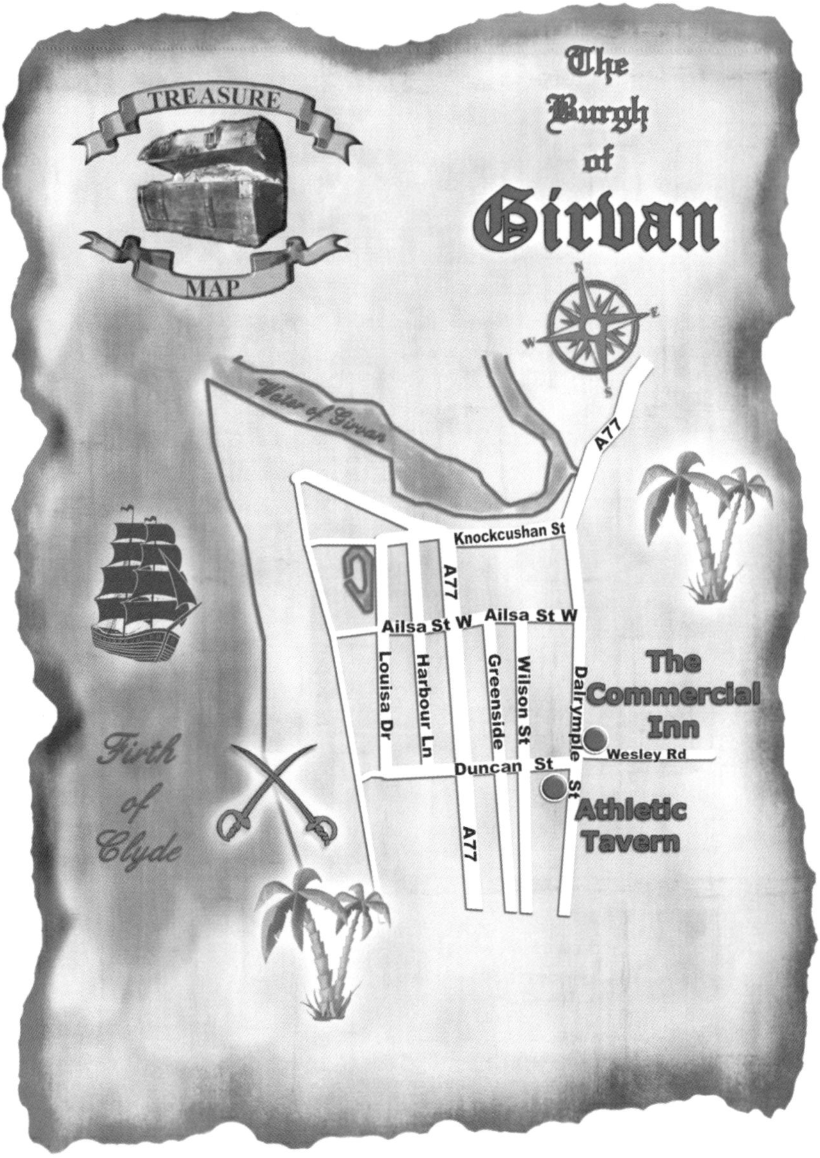
TREASURE
MAP
The Burgh of Girvan
N
E
S
W
Water of Girvan
A77
Knockcushan St
A77
Ailsa St W
Ailsa St W
Louisa Dr
Harbour Ln
Greenside
Wilson St
Dalrymple St
The Commercial Inn
Wesley Rd
Duncan St
Athletic Tavern
A77
Firth of Clyde

John; ***The Journey:*** Girvan is one of the three or four destinations which we can get to avoiding the journey into Glasgow. Today it's the X16 to Ayr then a local bus down to Girvan. That's the plan anyway!

Many years ago I visited Girvan a couple of times on golf outings. The unusual thing I remember about the course is that it is an 18 hole course. This is not unusual. What is, is that the first half of the course is links, then I think you go under the railway line, and the back nine is a parkland course. To most of you this is the most boring thing I have ever written, and that's going some. But to the golfers who have had the pleasure of playing Girvan, this fact will bring back memories of times gone by. You've got to admit, I'm full of it!

Craig had phoned me the night before to tell me of his concerns about the X16 timetable. 'Why were you checking it out, when that's my job?' I asked him. He told me he worries about my ability to read a timetable. Cheeky bugger! I've had no foul ups on the timetable front recently, I think! (I didn't actually say bugger).

Everything was fine, and we got on the X16 at our bus station at the back of nine. Craig insisted that I ask the driver if we were going to Ayr without changing buses. Suddenly I'm in charge of transport again. The driver assured me it was straight to Ayr, and he carried out his promise without any problems.

We arrived in Ayr Bus Station right on time at 10.17am, so we only had three minutes to catch our wee bus to Girvan. As far as I could make out from the timetable, the 10.20am bus was a number 58, but if we missed it, there was a number 60 at 10.50am, both going to Girvan. This was a worry. Why the number change?

At the bus station we found the stance for both the 58 and 60. Checking the details at the stop, they both went to some of the same places, but seemed to split up at Maybole. I had no time to work out where they actually went as the 58 turned up and on we got. I asked the driver if both buses took the same time. He told me that the No. 60 took five minutes less, but we would to wait half an hour for it. Even I could instantly work out that the 58 was the answer, and off we went.

The journey time was scheduled to take about an hour and five minutes, and as we headed out of Ayr towards Maybole, I couldn't fathom why it was going to take so long. I had forgotten about the 'LB' (Lazy B******) factor, which really annoys me. Now before I start my rant, I'm all for buses taking a roundabout route and visiting smaller towns and villages. This is what buses should be doing. But let me give you an example of one of today's 'LB' excursions, it happened when we reached Maybole.

The timetable shows that at Maybole the bus takes a left to go to Girvan via Dailly and other tiny hamlets. Now I am fine with that, it is a great idea. But what happens in Maybole is that the bus goes about 50 yards past its left turn, turns right, goes about 200 yards up a slope, turns right again, goes another couple of hundred yards, turns right again and goes back down to the main road to start the run to Dailly. During the LB detour, it disrupts local traffic and stops twice, picking up about one person. What's the point?

If it missed out that detour, it would save about 10 minutes, traffic congestion, some fuel, and more importantly, Craig having to listen to my rants. The only downside is that about two or three people would have to walk an extra 200 yards down to the main street. Now if the population of Maybole are up in arms about my comments, I am sorry and withdraw them. By the way, Craig was really fed up with my ranting at this, and a later LB detour. Mind you, he got his own back just before we got to Girvan when we detoured into a big building, and I started to complain before having a look up. I'm sure he will fill you in on my comments.

Our bus dropped us off at the harbour, although if we had stayed on the bus, it would have dropped us right outside the pub where we ended up, after a 15 minute walk via the beach. My reputation as a route planner was in tatters again. I will let Craig take it from here and tell you about our day drinking and digging for treasure.

Craig; *The day's Bars and Beaches;* Back in the dim and distant past, when I was a boy, Girvan was seen by many as a rather exotic destination. School trips and bus tours were the only holidays we ever got back then, and Girvan was always the most popular place to visit. It had everything: rowing boats, motor boats and a big Woolworth's store; what more could a bus-load of school kids ever want? Sadly a lot of the old magic has disappeared in the intervening years; even Woolworth's has gone.

We have of course visited Girvan before on our tour of Scottish pubs, and to be honest I wasn't really looking forward to repeating the experience. It was only when I discovered that there were a couple of pubs on Dalrymple Street that we hadn't seen before that I began to think it may be a reasonable day out after all.

John is forever going on about me complaining about various things, but on today's trip the boot was very much on the other foot. As soon as the bus from Ayr turned off the main road to visit some of the smaller towns along the route he started on what was to become a major rant. By the time we reached the outskirts of Girvan his face was turning purple with rage.

When the bus turned off into one last side road I thought he was going to pass out. While he was fizzing away at another unnecessary stop I pointed to the sign above the door of the building we had stopped outside. The relevant part of the sign declared that we had stopped right outside Girvan's Community Hospital. He was too far gone to take back anything he had said about the lazy passengers not willing to walk the length of themselves to catch a bus. However when I told him he should go and have a word with the wee old woman trying to get her wheelchair onto the bus, he did at least stop moaning.

It was my turn to complain a few minutes later, when the journey planner insisted that we get off at what turned out to be the wrong bus stop.

We have been doing this buzzing around the country for long enough now that I have come to expect the odd planning aberration on John's part, but I feel that I would be letting the side down if I didn't complain, accuse or generally take the piss out of him when he buggers things up. So after a long and pointless walk along the seafront we eventually found our way up to Dalrymple Street. In fact, we found the bus stop we should have gotten off at in the first place. It has thoughtfully been placed right outside one of the pubs we had decided to visit. In fact, the pubs are so close together that it was a toss of the coin to see which one we tried first.

The Commercial Inn, Girvan

The winner was The *Commercial Inn.* It is in an old sandstone building and is a real traditional-looking pub. I am happy to say that it is the same inside. The bar in this place would not be out of place in any small town in Scotland, especially if it happened to be the mid-1950s. The three flat screen tellies were a bit of an issue, but the sound was turned down so we decided not to notice them. What was noticeable however it was a total lack of carpets in the place; John was positively delighted.

Obviously we have no idea what the place is like at night or on the weekend, but just by the look of the bar we were confident that no women or weans frequent *The Commercial bar.* There is a small lounge at the back of the pub just in case any such people ever do turn up. We had only been in the place long enough to get our elbows onto the bar before one of the customers started talking to us. Malcolm Campbell and his pal John McIsaac were sitting on stools at the top end of the bar and were keen to find out who we were and what brought us to Girvan.

John McIsaac and Malcolm Campbell

I have to say that the people tend to get rather odd expressions on their faces when we tell them that we are not only doing a bit of metal detecting, but also writing a book about our experiences. Once again John felt the need to get a couple of books out to prove that we were not talking keech.

Malcolm told us that he was originally from Glasgow and had moved down to Girvan 20 odd years ago. He said that he had represented Glasgow at bowling championships and had even had a trial for the Scottish National squad.

There is an old saying about blowing your own trumpet because if you don't nobody else will. Malcolm has obviously heard of that particular one, as he went on at length about how good a bowler he had been. One of other customers shouted over that he had probably also won a few gold medals for modesty. Malcolm didn't even pause for breath as he went on to say that he would have been even more successful if he hadn’t injured his right arm many years ago. His pal John muttered something to the effect that he didn’t know about the injury stopping him from bowling but it certainly slowed him down paying for a round.

I was trying to work out who Malcolm reminded me of when it dawned on me that I was standing right next to the man. Although John is originally from Govan while Malcolm is a former Dennistoun boy, their daft Glasgow patter was strikingly familiar.

After Malcolm and John left to get their buses home, from the conveniently located bus stops outside the pub, we got talking to another of the *Commercial’s* regulars. Murdoch (Murdy) McLean is a victim of Thalidomide. This drug was prescribed widely for pregnant women in the 1960s. It was meant to lessen the effects of morning sickness. What it did was cause catastrophic damage to the unborn child. Murdy is badly affected, but he doesn't let that stop him from leading a normal life. Like the rest of us he enjoys a few beers and the daft patter you can only find a good old-fashioned Scottish pub.

We were chatting about our exploits on the different beaches we had visited and I suggested that John's biggest success with the metal detector had been finding the metal in his own hip replacement. That got a bit of a laugh from the company but it gave Murdy an idea. He came up with a challenge for us. It seems that a while ago he had a rod inserted into his leg because of a bad break, but he wasn't sure how long the rod was or even if it was metal. He bet us that we couldn't locate the rod. Actually I think he just wanted a look at our detector.

John discovers Murdy in The Commercial

John immediately got the small handheld detector out and started scanning Murdy's leg. There was not the slightest sound from the detector. To put it mildly, Murdy and the rest of the pub customers were less than impressed with our efforts. Even the pub owner, the aptly named George Beverage, joined in on the ridicule.

That was it, I had had enough! It was time to get the big guns out. Just to be clear, by big guns I mean the *Garrett Ace 150.* It took me a few minutes to build it up, as we dismantle it after use to get it into the equipment bag. Unfortunately this delay just raised the level of the mocking we had to endure.

Once the detector was built and ready it occurred to me that what seems like a good idea to a few well-oiled bar-flies might not seem quite so hilarious to a sober visitor. To any outsider who happened to stroll into *The Commercial* the whole thing might be seen as in poor taste or even insulting to the disabled. That phrase struck a chord with me: poor taste and insulting, there was only one man for this job. I handed the detector to John, telling him that since it was my camera I would have to take the pictures.

Fortunately it was a bit of a slow day in the pub and no new customers came in while we were getting up to this nonsense. Incidentally, we did find the metal rod and then discovered that John hadn't actually switched on the small detector in the first place.

Andy Capp takes in the view

Down on the beach we had a lot less setting up to do than usual as I had kept the detector assembled after using it in the pub. John said that I looked daft walking down the road with it under my arm. But I simply reminded him of what he had been doing with it a few minutes earlier and he shut up.

After having our sandwiches we set about scanning an area of the beach that we had marked out. Almost immediately I got a hit. It was amazing; we had found our first ever coins.

There were four of them and I could tell that they were coins from the Elizabethan period. Unfortunately the Elizabeth in question is the one who continues to reign over us.

We had found two twenty pence pieces and a pound coin but

to go by John's reaction you would have thought we had found a lost treasure trove. He was dancing about like the main character in the film 'City Slickers', just after he had found the gold.

Eventually I managed to calm him down and we continued searching the beach. During one of his turns at detecting, John got a really strong signal and straight away he announced that we had probably found the rest of the coin horde from earlier. We hadn't!

The search continued, with me sweeping the detector over the sand and John digging like a demented man every time the signal went off. After a few false alarms we found what looked like a piece of drainage pipe, or at least that's what it looked like to me. As expected John disagreed with my assessment. He claimed that it had to be from a sunken battleship or maybe even part of his fantasy submarine. If he is right about all of these 'ship parts' we keep finding it is no wonder that the British Navy is no longer the force it once was.

One of these days it won't be an old drainage pipe we find, it will be a fully active sewerage pipe, then 'the you know what' really will hit the fan.

We also found what looked like a silver bullet. It is usually John who comes up with the 'interesting' interpretations of the articles we find but this thing really did look like a silver bullet.

The only logical conclusions I could come to as an explanation for it being on Girvan's beach were worthy of any the weird and wonderful ideas John has ever come up with. Conclusion number one: the beach had, in recent times, been visited by the Lone Ranger. Conclusion number two: somewhere in the back streets of Girvan a wounded werewolf is stalking the town's residents.

Having spent some time down by the harbour I would have to say that a werewolf, wounded or otherwise, might not stand out too much in the crowd.

John claims that the same would be true over in the East End of Glasgow, where your average werewolf could pass a few hours down the pub without causing any upset. But, a Lone Ranger might not have such a quiet night.

To round off our day we decided to go back up the road, and this time visit the pub across the road from *The Commercial. The Athletic Tavern* looks like the kind of pub we would like, old but well-kempt. However, inside it was a bit of a let-down. It is mostly traditional but, for some reason, someone has seen fit to have the bar area and gantry redesigned by IKEA.

In my humble opinion bars should never be built using white pine, unless of course the idea is to get rid of the beer guzzling masses and replace them with the Prosecco crowd. If that was the idea here, it hasn't worked.

We didn't get a chance to talk to any of the pub's patrons but, to be fair, the horse racing was on the telly and everybody seemed to have a financial interest in the outcome of every race.

We made our way back to *The Commercial*. After all it is perfectly situated across the road from our bus stop.

The trip back up from Girvan was uneventful and an awful lot quieter than the trip down. This was because the bus took the coastal route which had fewer stops and John was still embarrassed about his earlier behaviour.

This had been a much better trip than we thought it would be. After all, we had at last found a horde of coins. The fact that their total cash value would just about get you a half pint of Tennent's Lager is neither here nor there.

John; A *review of the day;* I really enjoyed my hour or so on Girvan Beach. Apart from the cash, we found what I'm sure you will agree, looking at the picture, is a small silver bullet. I've no idea how it got to Girvan, but there you are. The big curved piece of anciend metal is obviously from some sunken ship, probably a naval vessel. If anyone has any other ideas, apart from me being daft, please write to us.

As Craig will have told you, we visited two pubs. The first one, *The Commercial Inn,* is a brilliant, traditional man's pub. Great bar and staff, and the customers were good company. Mainly old guys like ourselves. The second bar we visited briefly was *The Athletic Tavern.* This pub lacks atmosphere. It was like being in your living room, and everyone in the bar, including the barman, was engrossed in the horse racing, which is fine if you are into the geegees, which we are not.

On the way back up the road, we got the No. 60, which took the coast road to Ayr, passing old haunts like Turnberry, where I bored Craig with my tales of staying and playing there in the old days. Craig reckoned that I would like it even more, now it is owned by someone in line with my political leanings, Donald Trump. I told him he was exaggerating, and I would have him hanged if he did not retract his statement. He didn't!

There were a couple of 'LBs' on the journey back to Girvan, but the scenery is brilliant and well worth the trip.

We got the X16 at five o'clock and by the time we were leaving Kilmarnock it was lashing with rain, and it continued all the way back to EK. I texted Kate and arranged for her to pick us up at EK bus station. I allowed us an extra 40 minutes for a couple in the pub at the bus station. We were developing a thirst after being off the drink for over two hours. They went down like nectar.

So ended our day (or hour) on the beach in Girvan. It's amazing what you can find in such a short time, and I'm sure we will be millionaires by the end of the book.

Today' s finds;

John's thoughts on today's finds;

It doesn't get any better. You'll see from the photograph above that the items found can only be a silver bullet and some other ancient items from some sunken ship.

Craig's thoughts on today's finds;

Today's finds were quite varied and I particularly enjoyed finding the coins. Although we didn't start out looking for valuables it was really exciting when the detector signalled that there were coins lying under the sand. Of course it would have been much better if the coins had been a bit older; a couple of centuries perhaps.

How to get to Girvan Beach
(by Bus from Buchanan Street)

Citylink No. 923 bus to Stranraer will drop you off in Girvan. Book to ensure seat. Takes just over an hour and a half.
From EK it's the X16 to Ayr then a No. 58 or 60 to Girvan, a bus every half hour which takes about an hour.

Portobello Beach (Edinburgh)

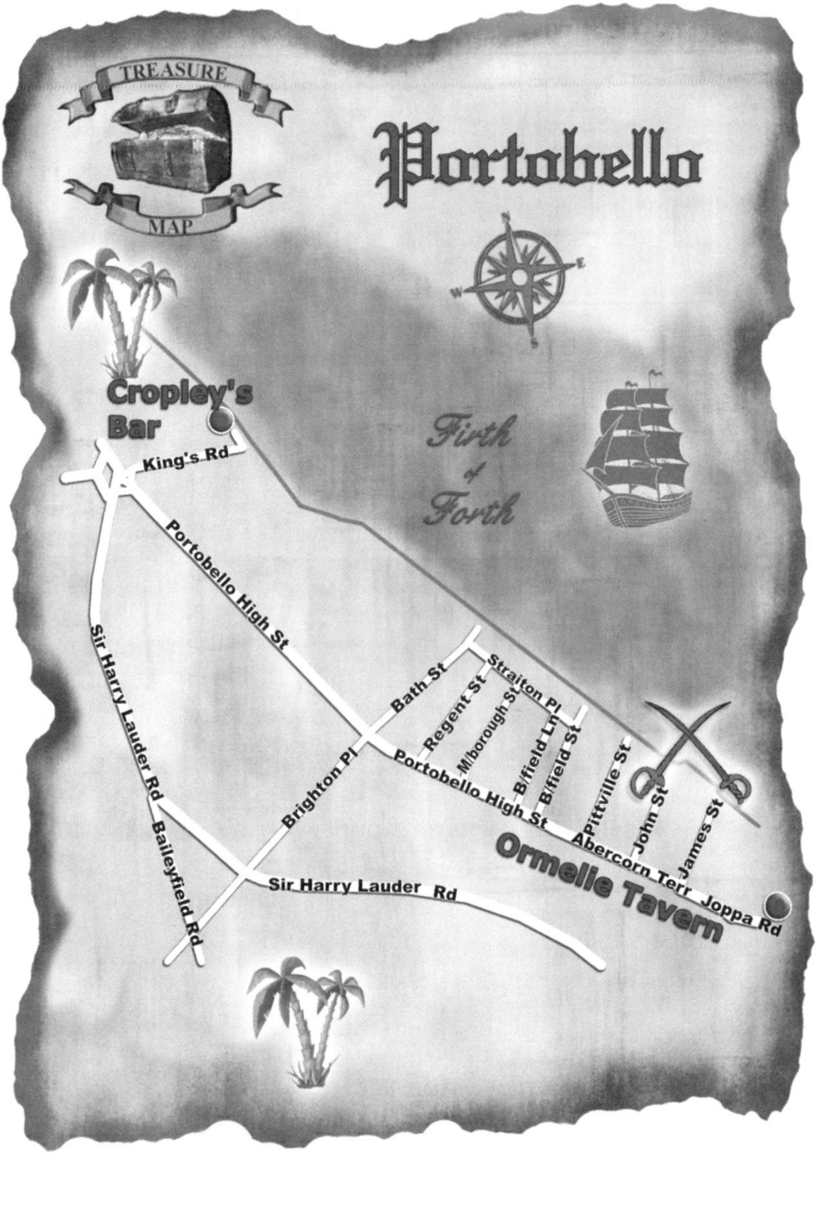

John: ***the Journey.*** I must start by saying that I had no idea where Portobello was. I thought it was in the East of Scotland somewhere, because I had never heard of it in the West. Craig was amazed at my ignorance, and was worried about my ability to organise a journey to a place I did not know. I assured him I would soon be on top of it and we would get there no problem. He was not convinced.

I was surprised to find out that it was in Edinburgh, and near the centre at that. I never think of our capital city having beaches, a castle and trams yes, but not any beaches.

On paper it was a fairly straightforward journey. The 900 bus to Princes Street-and they leave every 15 minutes-then a bus down to the beach. What could be simpler!

The journey into Buchanan Street bus station was straightforward, and I even showed Craig a shortcut through the Shopping Centre at the top of Buchanan Street, cutting through John Lewis and coming out right at the Bus Station. This saved us a lot of walking, mainly uphill, but Craig showed no appreciation. He even slagged me off for knowing my way through shops. You can't win.

On the bus to Edinburgh I asked Craig if he knew anything about Portobello. I know he always checks out the places we are visiting on the web. An interesting fact he let slip was that Portobello used to be called Frigatemuir. Beaches and warships are two of my favourite things, so I was sure we would find some valuable pieces of history on the beach that had been washed ashore from sunken frigates, or any other ships for that matter.

We got off the 900 in the bus station in Edinburgh. This is not where I had planned to get off, but Craig was adamant that we should get our next bus, the number 26, from just outside the bus Station on York Street. I was disappointed when this turned out to be the right decision.

The one problem we had was crossing York Street outside the Bus Station. Edinburgh trams pass this junction on their way to their terminus, which is along at the end of York Street, and not in Leith as was originally planned. Anyway, have you ever tried to cross a street in Edinburgh on which the trams pass? If you do the right thing and wait for the 'green man', you will be there all day. Because of Craig's lack of acceleration due to his bad feet, we had to wait. We missed two No.26s while we waited. Craig claimed it was only one, and that we would have missed it anyway.

There was a wee hiccup before we got to our destination. A stop before we were due to get off, the bus broke down. We got on the replacement bus as Craig refused to walk one stop, especially as it was not his fault. We duly got off at the next stop, only to discover that Craig had missed a stop on the Google Map thing, so we ended up having a wee walk after all, before getting to the pub Craig had picked out for our first port of call. And what a great pub it was.

Craig: *Today's Beaches and Bars.* Portobello was once a place the good people of Edinburgh flocked to when they wanted a beach holiday. In more recent times Portobello's outdoor swimming pool was well attended by those hardy types who have no fear of frostbite. In the early 1950s one of the lifeguards at the pool was none other than Sean Connery.

Apparently there was a permanent funfair and various amusement arcades along the prom. Obviously that was a long time ago, before the advent of foreign package holidays and a requirement to see the sun at some point in a two week break from work.

The heyday of Portobello as a visitor attraction may well be over, but there is still a two mile stretch of sand to attract the avid metal detectorists. Surely, somewhere in that vast area of sand there must be treasures just waiting to be found.

The area where Portobello now stands was a fairly desolate place known as Friggate Muir. It was an ideal location for seamen to ply their trade, especially those who preferred to avoid Britain's hefty import taxes.

At some time in the 1740s a local sailor built a cottage in the area and named it Portobello Hut. This was in honour of the 1739 capture of Porto Bello in Panama by the British navy. Eventually, others built homes beside the cottage and, as happens so often nowadays, the locals decided their village deserved a posher name. The name Portobello was therefore adopted. Given it had been known up until then as Friggate Muir I can't say I blame them.

I couldn't quite understand why John got so excited when I suggested visiting Portobello for our next day out. We had been chatting on the phone when I came up with the idea and I thought the line had gone dead for a few seconds before he managed to mumble a few words of agreement.

It was later in the day that I found out that he thought that we were taking the old metal detector overseas. Kate, his long suffering wife told me that he was on the point of checking his passport, before she put him right by explaining that we were in fact just nipping across to Edinburgh.

Actually I would have been happier if Edinburgh hadn't been mentioned. He gets a bit excited when it is brought up in conversation, as he has a thing about the tram system over there.

I think he has probably laid eyes on the trams twice in his life, but to listen to the man you would think that he had personally been made to pay for the whole system himself.

There is no denying that the track-laying process was a bit of a fiasco, but John can, and does, rant on and on about this squandering of public cash, if given half a chance.

He only stopped his latest rant when we boarded our bus out to Portobello and he once again realised that he didn't know where he was going.

The bus was so crowded that we had to go upstairs for a seat. That is just fine when you are about ten years old, but when you are getting on a bit and the arthritis is kicking in, it's not quite so much fun. All of that shoogling about and random braking make going up and down the stairs a bit of an adventure.

This particular bus trip became a somewhat traumatic affair. I had used my phone's sat-nav to pinpoint the exact point in Joppa Road we needed to get to but, unfortunately fate was not on our side.

The bus stopped about a quarter of a mile short of where we intended getting off. It seemed to be sitting there a bit longer than normal, but, being strangers to the east coast and not knowing the local customs and traditions we didn't immediately see a problem.

Even when most of the passengers got off the bus we didn't suspect a thing. Fortunately for us one of those passengers obviously saw that we were not natives of 'Porty' and took pity on us. He told us that we needed to get off the bus as it had broken down.

There must be some sort of special Edinburgh code for such occasions as I'm pretty sure that the driver never said a word to anyone about any breakdown.

Halfway down the stairs I overheard someone say that there had been a bad oil leak from the engine. This seemed to galvanise the rest of the passengers into action and they made a dash for the stairs. At that precise moment my phone rang. It is only human nature to reach for your phone when you hear it ring, no matter what is happening around you. I nearly landed face first onto the platform, but I did manage to save my phone from damage.

We had to change buses and in the confusion we managed to get off that bus at the wrong stop, leaving us a fair walk to our first pub of the day.

Although technically *The Ormelie Tavern* can't really be described as a beach bar, I had decided that we needed to start off our visit to Portobello with a drink in a good old-fashioned Scottish pub.

I had checked it out on the internet and it looked good. Of

course there is often a big difference between the outside and the inside of a pub. Many a grand façade has turned out to be just exactly that: Victorian architecture outside and like something out of a science fiction film on the inside.

I'm happy to report that *The Ormelie Tavern* turned out to be even better inside than out. It was so good in fact that John forgot to keep harping on about everything that had gone wrong so far that day.

Jennie, behind the bar in The Ormelie

The Ormelie is just the kind of pub we like; that's the reason I chose it. The two 'Beach Bars' we were supposed to visit couldn't really match up to our exacting standards. I had checked them out on my computer and it was obvious to me that *The Dalriada and Cropley's Bar* were far removed from our favoured, bog standard, Scottish boozer.

Just in case they were so bad that we wouldn't want to stay in them, as unlikely as that sounds, starting our day off with a good old-fashioned, no frills, no 'plooky' faced weans behind the bar ignoring us, pub experience, seemed like a sensible idea.

The Ormelie just felt comfortable to me. As soon as we walked into the place we felt right at home. It's a fair size inside and it is spotless.

We found a couple of empty stools and settled down for a quiet beer or three. That's not what we got, thanks to a trio of good natured hecklers who were sitting at the top end of the bar. We had started chatting to the barmaid, Jennie Gorrie, but we hardly managed to complete a sentence without some vocal interruption from the auld yins at the end of the bar.

The three wise men: William Urquhart, Tam McIntyre and Derrick Gunn

John was explaining to Jennie that we were out working on our seventh book. In telling people what we get up to on our days out he tends to go into a lot of unnecessary detail. Why he believes people would be interested in the composition of his sandwiches is anyone's guess. Once again he was going on about how much he loved his corned beef pieces, this time for Jennie's benefit. I think she was humouring him when she asked if he ever thought of adding some lettuce or finely sliced tomatoes to the corned beef.

Before he could answer her, one of the three wise men

shouted over, “No chance! He’s from Glasgow, what would he know about vegetables?”

When they heard that we intended to do a bit of metal detecting down on the beach the old guys got even louder. One of them, Tam McIntyre I think, told us that we had absolutely no chance of finding anything on the beach. Apparently he knew for a fact that there had been a bloke down there with a detector quite recently, so there was no point in us even trying.

At the time I had only seen photographs of Portobello beach, but it looked fairly large to me, more than enough sand for a couple of detectorists.

I did think of explaining this to Tam, but as John seemed to be trying to flog him a book I decided to keep my expert knowledge of beaches to myself. The negotiations were at a tricky stage, with Tam trying to work out if it would be cheaper to buy us a round of drinks or just pay the asking price for the book.

The excitement was too much for me so I went for a wander around the pub. That was when I came across a rather strange photograph through in the lounge area. It was a picture of a diver in full dry suit and pressure helmet. The odd thing was, the diver wasn’t sitting on the edge of a boat, about to slip over the side and down into the waters of the North Sea. He was standing in the middle of Joppa Road, just outside the pub.

Jennie explained that the basement of the pub and those of the houses next to it, were being flooded on a regular basis. Since the pub, and its basement, is well above any possible tidal flooding, suspicion fell upon old mine workings which stretch out under The Firth of Forth.

To check it out, a diver had to be lowered into the sewer pipes. That’s not exactly the glitzy, glamorous image I had of being a professional deep-sea diver. I wonder if this diver thought he would end up swimming through crap for a living when he graduated from diving school.

I happened to mention to a chap at the bar that we were

going to visit *Cropley's bar* which is at the other end of Portobello. It is less than a stone's throw from the beach which qualified it as one of the few real beach bars in Scotland.

However I got the distinct impression that he wasn't too keen on my choice of pub, when he asked me if I had ever actually seen the pub. I said that I had seen pictures online but had never been in the place. I had to admit that it did look a bit odd as far as normal pubs go, but I was looking forward to having a pint there.

Over my many years of experience in visiting pubs I have seen some rather odd building converted into pubs. These have included churches, industrial buildings and, on one memorable occasion, a hut, but until now I have never heard of a public toilet being turned into a boozer.

Don't get me wrong, I have been in some pubs that looked a bit like toilets; I have even been in some that smell as if they have been used as toilets, but never in one that actually used to be a genuine public loo.

I decided not to tell John about the former use of *Cropley's,* because I knew that he would have a field day with the knowledge. Listening to his jokes and puns for the rest of the day was more than I was prepared to take. His banter tends to be a bit toilet based at the best of times; so there was no point feeding him any easy material.

We got a rousing send off from the *Ormelie* customers, especially all the guys at the end of the bar. That was a bit wasted when John realised that he had left his notebook on the bar and had to sneak back in to get it.

It was a fairly short walk from the pub down to the Portobello beach. When we got there I was amazed at the length of it. There must be more than two miles of clean, golden sand there. Using all my metal detecting experience I estimated that it would take us a couple of hundred years to scan the entire beach. Since we only had about an hour to spend there we had to be quite selective.

Once we found a likely spot we sat down to have our lunch. We find that eating our pieces before we start chucking large amounts of sand around makes for a more enjoyable meal.

Usually it is me who does all the technical work when we are out on the beach. It's easier that way, as John has a bit of a history with things mechanical: they tend to bite him. The last time I asked him to assemble our special shovel it was out of commission for a couple of weeks.

However, every now and then, he does offer to do some of this work, but I can usually come up with an excuse to put him off. Unfortunately I was a bit too slow this time. He got his hands on the detector while I was still finishing off my sandwiches.

The detector is stored in three pieces and has to be put together in an exact order, but I wouldn't say it was overly complicated. I decided to let him get on with it; what could possibly go wrong?

I spent my time getting my camera ready, but when I looked back over to where he was, I could see that he was trying to attach the handle of my walking stick to the top of the metal detector. I did try to explain that he was making an arse of things, but, to be honest, it was quicker just taking it from him and doing it myself.

It only took a few minutes to do and I had just finished when I heard him say that that he thought he might have broken the shovel again.

All of this might just be a clever ruse to get me to do all of the donkey work, but the smart money is on him being 'haunless'. To be on the safe side I thought it might be wise to put him in charge of the plastic sieve.

We had barely started scanning the beach when a small boy wandered over to see what we were doing. He then proceeded to get in our way, trip over the detector and generally get right up our noses. The child was out of control.

After many discussions on the subject, I can safely say that neither John nor myself can be bothered with noisy weans. But spoiled wee brats are a completely different category altogether. The one good thing was, this particular small waste of space had the attention span of a goldfish. When nothing was found after five minutes, he wandered off to make someone else's life a misery.

John suggested that maybe it would be a good idea if we went over and gave his 'Mummy', who had been on the phone all this time, a good slap, 'just to sharpen her parenting skills'. He didn't use those exact words, but I knew what he meant. Instead of straightening out the kid's future we decided to get on with searching the beach.

In no time at all we found a coin and a few rusty nails. The coin was probably no more than ten years old, but, according to John, the nails were ancient. He reckoned they might be from an old navy warship. It didn't seem to occur to him that they could be from some other source: like the old wooden fence we were standing next to, which was being held together by some old rusty nails.

A few minutes later we got another strong signal from the detector. It really is quite exciting when we get such a strong indication. Whatever it was, it was big. John started digging and the object seemed to get bigger and bigger. So it was a great disappointment when he eventually revealed that what he had found was a large plank of wood. It had some nails in it which had obviously given us the signal.

It goes without saying that John saw something other than an old piece of driftwood. He claimed that for all we knew, this piece of wood could have come from the same place as the nails we had found: the warship.

I don't know if it was the effects of the sea air or the alcohol I had supped earlier, but I suggested that there was a good chance that this bit of planking could have come from the original hut from which Portobello took its name.

That was a mistake. I should really be more careful about encouraging John's imaginings. I had to stop him from trying to get the plank into our kit bag to bring it home. To placate him I said that I would take a picture of it instead. He wasn't too pleased by this but, when I said he could be in the photo as well, he dropped his objections.

Two short planks on Portobello beach

There was no way he could resist that offer. We have been to more than 600 pubs over the years we have been writing these books, and I am prepared to bet that I have pictures of John, mugging it up for the camera outside most of them.

Once I had taken the photo we decided that it was time to pack up and start looking for our first 'real' beach bar of the day. I had found *The Dalriada* while doing my online research on Portobello. On its web site the pub claims to be Edinburgh's bar on the beach, but to be honest it doesn't really look like anyone's idea of an exotic beach front watering hole.

In fact it looks like a fine example of a traditional Victorian town house, built when towers and turrets were seen as a fashionable addition to seaside homes.

I was looking forward to visiting it. In their advert they claim to have a cosy cider garden and, since I have never heard of such a thing, I was keen on finding out exactly what a cider garden looked like. However, some things are just not meant to be.

Despite having a map of the area, we couldn't find *The Dalriada*. John suggested that, given the way things are nowadays, with so many pubs closing down, perhaps this one had also ceased trading. Actually I think he just didn't fancy visiting a pub that was so upmarket that it had its own cider garden.

We wandered around for another ten minutes or so, before I admitted defeat and agreed to head back up to the bus stop on the main road.

As soon as I set eyes on *Cropley's,* it was very obvious that it had started out as something other than a pub. It is a very odd shaped building and I had been told that it had once been a public toilet. I would have to say that it must have been a very impressive one in its day.

Whoever did the conversion has made a very good job of it, but then, I suppose, there wouldn't be a lot of the original interior you could re-use. The decor is a bit on the modern side for my liking but, when you think about it, going for a really traditional effect would be a bit silly in such an odd-shaped building. It was such an odd shape that, at first, we couldn't find our way in. At one point John even tried to climb over the wall into the beer garden.

There were only a few customers in the bar, so we were quite surprised that it took so long for us to get served. The barman didn't seem too pleased to see us; he certainly wasn't in a hurry to take our order. Perhaps he overheard John treating me to even more of his toilet humour. I expect the poor man has heard it all before.

We have a bit of a piss up in Cropley's Bar

John was just about to order our second drink when it occurred to me that I should probably make some room for it with a quick trip to the gents. That turned out to be a little more difficult than it really should have; the door was locked.

I've never seen a combination lock on a toilet door before and I couldn't help but wonder how many 'little accidents' occur in *Cropley's* when enthusiastic beer drinkers get to this door, before realising that they've forgotten the combination.

I went back to the bar and asked the barman for the number but, instead of telling me, he came round the bar and keyed in the numbers himself. Maybe he thought I was too thick to work the mechanism, or he just doesn't trust strangers, but there was no way he was parting with that number.

It struck me as ironic that the owners of this former toilet had made it so difficult for their customers to go for a pee.

My theory about the barman not trusting strangers with the combination seemed to be proved true when I overheard him telling another customer the combination.

If you ever find yourself in *Cropley's* and feel the need to use the facilities, the number is 147.

So ended our Portobello adventure; we were better off by one 20p piece, a few rusty nails and a picture of two short planks on a beach. Not a bad day out.

A few days after our visit to Portobello I was looking through some of the pictures I had taken on the beach. In one of them, John can be seen sitting on the sea wall. It was only when I looked carefully at this photo that I noticed, in the background, the entrance to *The Dalriada*, our missing pub.

John: ***A review of the day.*** Portobello is a really nice town with a brilliant beach. I reckon the property must be worth a fortune, being so close to the centre of Edinburgh.

We had a smashing day. The first pub we were in, *The Ormelie Tavern* was a very good, the kind we like, and the staff and locals were great company. I even managed to get one of of them to buy a book. He offered £3 (the cover price is £9.99). I suppose this is generous for an Edinburgh man, but I told him I would give him the book for nothing if he bought us a round. This put him over £5 out of pocket. As this is more than we get after Waterstone's take their cut, I was well chuffed.

The pub we went into after our metal detecting, or treasure hunting, as I call it to annoy Craig, was called *Cropley's.* It was right on the promenade, with a beer garden overlooking the beach and Firth of Forth. I'm sure Craig has filled you in on its merits. Enough to say that at least it had a good view.

Our beachcombing started off slowly, only an old 20p coin and a couple of nails turning up. But then, wham! We uncovered a four feet long plank. There was no doubt in my mind where it came from and what it was. If you look at the photograph. I'm sure you will agree with my thoughts, which you will find under the photo.

We had a fine day out in Portobello. It is well worth a visit. The beach has a lovely prom and no road along it, so it would be safe for small children. Even though it's in Edinburgh, and not the West of Scotland, it is one of the best beaches I have visited.

The journey back to Glasgow was seamless, but as we were arriving at Buchanan Street, we got a message from my Kate letting us know that there were no trains running to East Kilbride because of the ongoing strike. This would mean walking down past George Square to get a No. 18. My bladder did not fancy an hour on the bus, and Craig's feet were louping.

I came up with the brilliant idea of getting the Hamilton Bus, which I was sure left from Buchanan Street and would drop us off in Rutherglen Main Street, where we could pick up an No. 18 to East Kilbride. This meant no walking for Craig and two short bus journeys, instead of one long one. Easier on the old bladder.

The idea worked perfectly, and we got a bus right away. We even had a quick pint in Rutherglen before getting our EK bus. I'm sure Craig will mention that we had a long wait for the 18. The man is never happy. Overall, a great day out.

John's thoughts on today's finds;

It is obvious to me that the plank we found, which measured about four feet long by around three inches deep, is a section of the deck from some sunken ship. It could even be from the Frigate that the town used to take its name from. Make your own decision.

Craig's thoughts on today's finds;

I had a hard time explaining to people that we had found a plank of wood by using a metal detector.

How to get to Portobello

(by Bus from Buchanan St. Bus Station)

The number 900 leaves Buchanan Street every 15 minutes and takes about an hour and a half to get to Edinburgh Bus Station. From York Street, just outside the station, get a number 26 bus which takes about 25 minutes to Portobello.

Dunbar

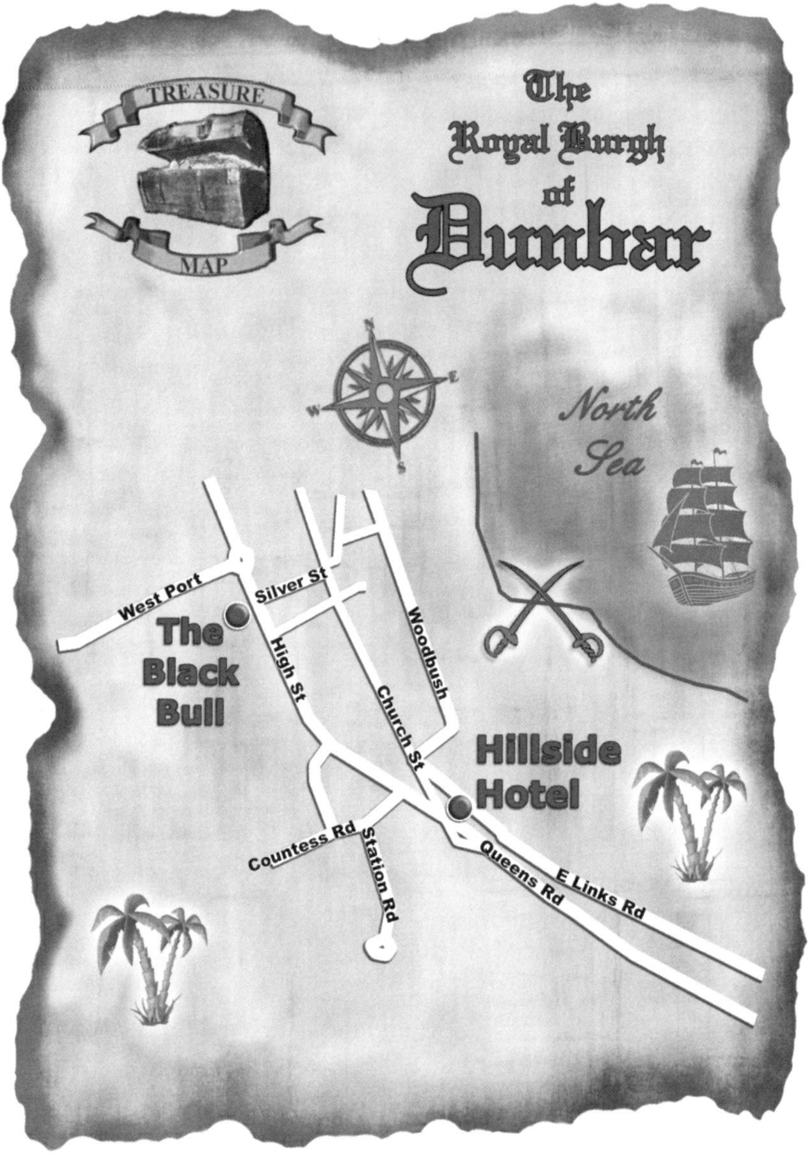
TREASURE
MAP
The Royal Burgh of Dunbar
N
E
W
S
North Sea
West Port
Silver St
The Black Bull
High St
Woodbush
Church St
Hillside Hotel
Countess Rd
Station Rd
Queens Rd
E Links Rd

John; ***The journey:*** Today's journey was one I did not fancy at all. The idea of going to Edinburgh is bad enough, but then having to make your way to North Berwick would be a nightmare. North Berwick was where we were planning to go. Craig was insistent that we should take in this neck of the woods, so the books would appeal to people in the East, (as if anyone in North Berwick is going to read the rubbish I write).

I went into the Traveline web page, and my worries were confirmed. Apart from the hour into Glasgow, it's an hour and a half on the bus to Edinburgh, then an hour and a quarter from Edinburgh to North Berwick. It would take us all day to get there!

Craig left me to do the organising. I was about an hour into this massive job when Craig phoned me to say that we were going to Dunbar! 'Why?', I asked. 'There's no pubs near the beach in North Berwick', came the reply.

He assured me that Dunbar, although looking further away on the map, took the same time to get to as North Berwick. How did he know this?

Could I do what I have done before and talk the tight-fisted Craig into opening his wallet and going by train. As I was looking at times from Queen Street to Edinburgh, it suddenly came to me that trains run from Glasgow Central to Edinburgh going via Motherwell. We could get the old 201 from outside Craig's house straight to Motherwell Railway Station, then get a train from there to Dunbar, via Edinburgh Waverley.

I was sure I could talk Craig into this idea. There would be almost no walking, and the journey by train would be almost two hours less, that's about six pints. I also said we would pay for the journey using the company card. That did it! We were off to Dunbar on the train, with the drinking allowed and everything.

I have been to Dunbar once before on a day's fishing trip with my neighbour Richard and a few of his friends. A couple of things I remember is that it had a nice main street with a few pubs. Another is that there is a huge seal called 'Sammy', who stays in the Harbour all day and comes right up to the boats with the top half of his body out of the water to beg for fish. By the size of him he is never refused. I must ask a local if he's still to the fore, and how do they know his name is Sammy?

While I was fishing that day, the gannetts were diving right next to our boat, going under the water to catch fish. It was an amazing sight. Then one of them dived right up against me and ended up caught on my hook. I damn well nearly guano'd myself. For the well-read among you, the Bass Rock is just off Dunbar and it is completely white. This is caused by the 100,000 or so gannetts that nest there and cover the rock with guano. I must be honest here and say that I am just assuming that guano is a 'birdy' name for shit. The story had a happy ending as the others on the boat managed to stop me running round in circles screaming, and they were able to release the bird unharmed, which is more than you could say about my undies.

After that riveting piece of historical drama, back to today's trip. I picked Craig up at 10am and our 201 took us right to Motherwell Rail Station. I was pleased when Craig proved that his memory is as bad as mine. He commented that he had never been to Motherwell before, followed ten seconds by him saying 'There's the *Horeshoe Bar,* remember we were in there'.

We got our day return tickets from a very helpful ticket man who came from the East (East of Scotland). There was no oldie discount, so our company card took a hammering. I didn't tell Craig the total as I knew it would spoil his day. The first part of his day was spoiled anyway as the train was very full and we were sitting apart, the problem for Craig was that he was surrounded by noisy kids. His face was like fizz.

It was a successful transfer of trains in Waverley Station, and we were soon enjoying the lovely run across to Dunbar. There was only one other passenger in our carriage. He was a big guy in shorts who looked as if he had had a wee refreshment already. I'll let Craig tell you about the second time we met him.

As we got near Dunbar, in brilliant sunshine, we passed The Bass Rock, still all covered in guano. Shortly after this trip I was talking to my wee sister Gillian and her husband Mark about the Bass Rock, and she told me that one day they were canoeing in that area and they couldn't get any closer than about a mile from the rock because of the smell from the guano. Hope this is of interest to my readers.

We arrived on time in Dunbar, still very refreshed, but gasping for a refreshment, so we wandered down the main street and into *The Black Bull,* a wee 'old man's' type of pub. I'll let Craig take it from here.

Craig; *Today's Beaches and Bars:* After a bit of dithering about we eventually agreed that our next outing would be to Dunbar. I had checked out the pubs in the town using my computer and I liked what I saw. Added to that, the beach look really good and, more importantly for me, it was just a short walk from the main street. All we had to do was get there.

Usually I am quite critical of John’s transport arrangements but, for once they were almost flawless. The only annoying thing was the lack of seating on the train from Motherwell to Edinburgh, but I don't suppose it would be fair to blame him for that.

I really didn't think the train would be busy as the journey from Central Station in Glasgow to Waverley Station in Edinburgh is not usually considered the main route between the two cities. Most Edinburgh trains leave from Queen Street station but the train we were waiting for was actually going all the way to Penzance.

Judging by the number of people hogging the seats, I can only assume that something really interesting must have been going on down in Cornwall.

By the time we got off the train in Dunbar there was only one item on our agenda: finding a pub. I had taken great care mapping out the shortest route to what looked like the best pubs, but it came as no surprise to me that John instinctively headed off in the wrong direction. I always add an extra five or 10 minutes travelling time so that I can shepherd him back onto the right track.

There were two pubs on High Street that I liked the look of, and by sheer good fortune, they were directly across the road from each other. Both *the Eagle Inn* and *the Black Bull* are traditional, substantial-looking Scottish pubs. In fact there was nothing we could see that would favour one over the other.

I quite fancied visiting *the Eagle Inn* for purely nostalgic reasons, not that I've ever actually been in that pub. In fact this was my first ever visit to Dunbar. I just wanted to see if it was anything like *the Eagle Inn* that I had started my drinking career in back in Auchinleck.

My *Eagle Inn* was a place of legend. It certainly wasn't for the squeamish. It was a place where boys became men, then older men and eventually, if they lived long enough, alkies. The chances of Dunbar's *Eagle* being anything like my old boyhood boozer was rather small. But comparing the differences might be fun

In the end John decided that we should try *the Black Bull* first, then move on to *the Eagle*. That sounded like the kind of plan I could live with, so we went in. We were rewarded with a good old-fashioned three sided bar with a traditional gantry. The ceiling is fairly low but that just added to the atmosphere of the place.

There were only two or three customers in the pub when we entered, which meant we had no difficulty finding a bar stool. I don't mind standing at the bar, obviously, but after a bit of a walk on a nice warm day, a bar stool and a cold pint is my idea of heaven. However, before I could even manage to put my rear end on the waiting barstool, my phone rang and I had to go outside to answer it.

I was only gone for about five minutes but by the time I got back into the bar John had sold a book to one of the customers. As you can imagine he was very pleased with himself because of that, but a minute later he was even more pleased

For a while now John has been swapping his beer for vodka. He claims that he is trying to lose weight and that sticking to vodka and soda works wonders. Personally I think he just wants to drink his booze a bit quicker. Anyway when he asked for a vodka he was stunned to hear that a single 25ml would cost him just a pound. The slimming campaign went out of the window almost immediately and he ordered a double. That set the pattern for the rest of the day.

After sampling a few cheap vodkas, John started reminiscing about his last visit to Dunbar. He had been on a fishing trip with some friends and from what I heard of their day out, there was quite a lot of booze on board the boat. In fact the phrase booze cruise was used to describe their day out.

John told our barman, Allan Nairn, that he had a vague recollections of a large seal trying to get onto his boat, while they were still in the harbour. I really thought he might have been hallucinating; he had after all claimed that he had caught a gannet on his fishing line earlier on the same trip. If that doesn't sound like the ravings of someone who had been on the grog all day then I'm very much mistaken.

Much to my surprise Allan confirmed that such a creature does indeed exist. He said that the seal was famous on the east coast. It is called Sammy the Seal and has been begging for fish in the harbour for years. In fact Allan said that there has been more than one Sammy the Seal over the years.

This confirmed my suspicions; Dunbar is a weird place

Our barman was keen to fill us in on some of Dunbar's history. It seems that within a few hundred yards of the pub is birthplace of John Muir the environmentalist and the man who inspired the American National Parks system. Not quite on the same scale, there is a country park just outside Dunbar named in honour of John Muir.

Over the years the town has seen its fair share of trouble often being burnt to the ground by invading armies. With such a strategic position on the east coast Dunbar has been fought over by the Scots and English many times.

One of the town's most notable visitors was Oliver Cromwell in 1650. He was in the town for the Battle of Dunbar, where his troops defeated an army of Scottish royalists.

John wasn't too interested in all of this history talk, but he perked up bit when the barman mentioned that Belhaven Brewery was located in the town. When he is not guzzling vodka, his favourite tipple is a pint of Belhaven Best.

We were joined at the bar by a very nice lady named Kim, who just happens to be the barman's mum. She told me that *the Black Bull* is without doubt the friendliest pub in Dunbar. It seems that a few years ago it was considered a bit of an old man's pub and stuck in the past, but since being taken over by the present owner a lot of younger people now frequent the place.

Allan Nairn and his mum Kim

It was however, two of the pub's older characters I talked to next. Mike Shaw and Robert Nelson were regulars in the pub and both of them have spent many years in the RNLI. Mike was a crewman aboard the Dunbar lifeboat, while Robert worked in the office.

I had to ask Robert, given his surname is Nelson, if he had never wanted to go out on the boat, but he said he hadn't been allowed to serve. The problem was he couldn't swim. I could see how that could be seen as a drawback, but Robert managed to turn it into an advantage. Every time the crew needed to practise rescuing a drowning man he found himself being flung overboard.

I suppose the fact that he was a non-swimmer added an element of authenticity to the exercise.

Robert Nelson and Mike Shaw

Mike told me that his friend, Noel White, was the longest serving coxswain in the RNLI. He was so well respected in the Institute that he was allowed to serve on any lifeboat in the UK. In fact whenever a relief crewman was needed anywhere in the country his was the first name on the list. The odd thing was, despite his high-profile, Noel could not read or write. He spent much of his time successfully covering up the fact. Noel died last year.

We were working our way through our second drink when a large and rather tipsy looking man came rumbling into the bar. I recognised him from the train earlier and at that time I reckoned that he had been on an extended bender and was making his way home. Since then he had obviously been doing the rounds of the local pubs.

His first question to the barman was unconnected to buying a drink. He wanted to know if he had been causing bother in the pub the night before and followed that up by asking if he was barred. After a bit of earnest pleading he was allowed a pint; but that was to be his limit.

Obviously that turned out to be nonsense; he was still there when we left. Before that however, he insisted on buying everyone in the pub a drink. I didn't mind the drink: it was the cuddling I wasn't too keen on. He staggered around the bar hugging each of the customers, even the ones who were trying to avoid him like the plague.

As I have often said, we really like no frills, old fashioned pubs, and in most respects *The Black Bull* fitted our requirements. It does however have a jukebox- a very modern jukebox. John is not the most technically savvy bloke in the world, in fact if it is anything more complicated than a clockwork toy he gets confused. There was only one reason I could think of for John suddenly becoming interested in using that very complicated machine, and that was to avoid the clutches of the over friendly drunk bloke. It didn't work.

We were joined at the bar by the pub's owner Andrew Soars. That was enough of an excuse for another round of drinks to be ordered. It began to look like we wouldn't be going across the road to *The Eagle Inn*.

Actually, I was beginning to think that we might not be doing any metal detecting either.

Andrew took over *The Bull* last year and he told us that the pub had a good reputation for the friendliness of both its customers and staff. I couldn't place his accent and had to ask him where he was originally from. He said that he gets asked that question a lot, and people are genuinely surprised to hear that he is from nearby Edinburgh. The mystery of the strange accent was solved when he revealed that he had been in the navy for many years.

Andrew Soars and Allan

With great effort I managed to convince John that it was time to go. They say that time and tide wait for no man and that was certainly true for us in Dunbar. We had wasted too much time enjoying the craic in the pub and the tide had come in while we were doing so.

Fortunately, we managed to find a stretch of sand still above the water. By my reckoning the sea would not come any further in, so we decided to have our lunch before getting the detector out. I thought it was a particularly good idea to get some food into John, as he had taken full advantage of the cheap booze in *the Bull.*

Although our day had started out so well, things definitely took a turn for the worse once we started scanning the beach. I was beginning to think that the people of Dunbar must be the neatest people I'd ever come across. The beach was very clean and any metal object which had been dropped there must have been picked up again. Suddenly the buzzer indicated that we had at last found something. After a few moments digging we uncovered the object we were searching for; it was a stone.

I was less than impressed but John insisted that it was a very special stone. He is either the most optimistic man on Earth or the alcohol has finally started to affect his brain. While we were stumbling about on the sand, failing to find anything remotely interesting, an older woman came over to talk to us. She had been doing a bit of beachcombing and had found some really nice pieces of ceramic tile.

That just made me feel worse; we would have been better off chucking the metal detector and just looking for shiny things down by the high water mark. This lady has been collecting stuff from the beach for many years and knew all of the best spots to find washed-up objects. Needless to say we were not standing on one of the spots.

We were thinking about cutting our losses and heading for another pub when I got another hit and it was a big hit. About six inches down in the sand we found a large metal object. It was so big that we couldn't find its edges. There was some sort of handle on it and I thought that we had maybe found a drain cover. The way our luck was running I would not have been too surprised if it had turned out that we had found a sewer pipe.

John, unsurprisingly, took a different view of what we had uncovered. He declared that we had found an unexploded mine. I suggested that if he really believed that this thing was an unexploded mine, it might be a good idea to stop hitting it with his metal shovel.

Since it was unlikely that we would find anything bigger than John's mine, we decided to pack up the detector and head for a nearby pub.

I had checked out the pubs nearest to the railway station. This was in an attempt to cut down the distance we would have to walk if, by some chance, we were carrying a large haul of valuables taken from the beach.

Obviously we didn't need any help carting our haul of goodies away from the sand. John's unexploded mine had been left for someone else to dig up, but it was good to be heading towards the station anyway. The name of the bar we were looking for was *the Hillside Hotel*. I thought that the name of the place suggested where we were likely to find it. John didn't get the connection and tried to head away from the rather obvious hill at whose foot we were standing.

Eventually I got the message across and we made our way up to the hotel. The only reason for choosing *the Hillside* was its closeness to the railway station, so we didn't really have much expectation of finding a decent boozer. However, we were pleasantly surprised to find a nice wee bar at the front of the hotel

I think there were only three other customers in the pub, but there were two people behind the bar serving. That has to be the best customer to staff ratio I have come across. It wasn't long before John was regaling the assembled company with stories of his adventures in metal detecting. And, for once, he did mention that I had been there when he had made some of his greatest discoveries. Eventually he got around to talking about what he had found on the beach, just down from the hotel.

When he finished this fairy tale, he was still the only person in Dunbar who thought that there was an unexploded mine on the beach. We were then treated to a true story about wartime mines by Stewart McKerrache, an older gent who was sitting at the bar.

It seems that during the war many mines were released into the waters around the fishing grounds in the North Sea. Many of these were British mines meant to defend strategic approaches to the harbours and other important sites. Others were possibly dropped into the sea by the Germans, who were known to get up to such tricks. Anyway it was vitally important that the fishing fleet was allowed to operate as normally as possible. But, with all those mines floating about, damage to fishing nets was unavoidable. To keep things running smoothly the government paid compensation to fisherman who produced any net, or portion of net, damaged beyond repair. Stewart told us that there wasn't a net in the fleet that hadn't been replaced several times.

Stewart McKerrache

The daft patter continued like this for some time. Behind the bar Tam Bradley and Rhona McLean kept the beer flowing and even joined in with some daft patter of their own. In fact Tam even claimed that Dunbar was the sunniest town in Scotland.

If I had a pint for every time a barman had claimed that his wee toon was either the sunniest, the driest or warmest place in the country, I would be pretty well oiled right now. Having said that, I suppose that one of them has to right, so, maybe Tam does know what he is talking about.

That is more than you can say about John. He insisted on questioning Rhona about her relationship with Tam. The poor girl didn't know where to look. She told him that they were just friends, but that was never going to satisfy John. It was like watching a particularly tacky dating show on the telly, with John playing the part of Jeremy Kyle.

Tam Bradey and Rhona McLean

Although she was a good sport about it all, I'm fairly sure she breathed a sigh of relief when we announced that it was time for us to leave.

Although we hadn't found any interesting items on the beach, not even an unexploded mine, we had found two really great pubs and some very nice people on our visit to Dunbar.

John had found his spiritual home, where vodka was just about as cheap as tap water, and drunk people insist on buying the drinks. Maybe one day I will go back there, just to check out *the Eagle Inn.*

John; *A review of the day:* We had a brilliant day in Dunbar. The weather was glorious, and so it should be. Dunbar is officially the sunniest place in Scotland. I found out that information from Tam Bradley in the *Hillside Hotel*. Another piece of information I was glad to hear was that 'Sammy' the Seal is still to fore and begging for fish from the local boats as usual. God knows what size he must be now. The harbour itself is quite small. Tam also assured me that the name Sammy was given to him by his mother!

We had a great time in both places we visited, especially *The Black Bull,* where the locals were as daft as us. Our visit there lasted a lot longer than planned and the walk up and down down till we found the beach was a nightmare in the sun.

Our detecting was fun and we had several talks with locals who all thought we were a bit mad.

The journey back to EK via Waverley and Motherwell passed in a flash, and we were home about two hours earlier than if we had taken the bus. Having said that, Dunbar is about the most awkward place to visit from EK, and our next trip will be back on our traditional mode of transport, the bus.

Johns thoughts on today's finds;

After a few false alarms, we came across a piece of black rock which got a good reading from our *Ace Garrett 150.* We have found a similar stone before so I'm beginning to think they may not be as valuable as I originally thought.

On the other hand, our main find of the day was a bumper. There is no doubt in my mind that what we found could be an old mine which has been dropped by a German plane during the war. Craig's claim that it could be part of the sewage system does not make sense as the handle part of the find is far too small to be part of a sewage system. We could not verify the find as Craig was too feart to tamper further with it in case it exploded! So much for it being part of a sewage pipe!

Craig's thoughts on today's find's:

Once again John's imagination got the better of him. There is absolutely no chance that the thing we found on the beach was a mine.

How to get to Dunbar
(by bus from Buchanan Street)

The number 900 to Edinburgh leaves every 15 minutes. When you get off the bus, go down into Leith Street, and the X6 to Dunbar leaves from stop JD.

(by train from Central Station)

Not difficult to explain. Go up to the ticket office and ask for a day return to Dunbar. It is a bit costly, mind you.

St. Andrews

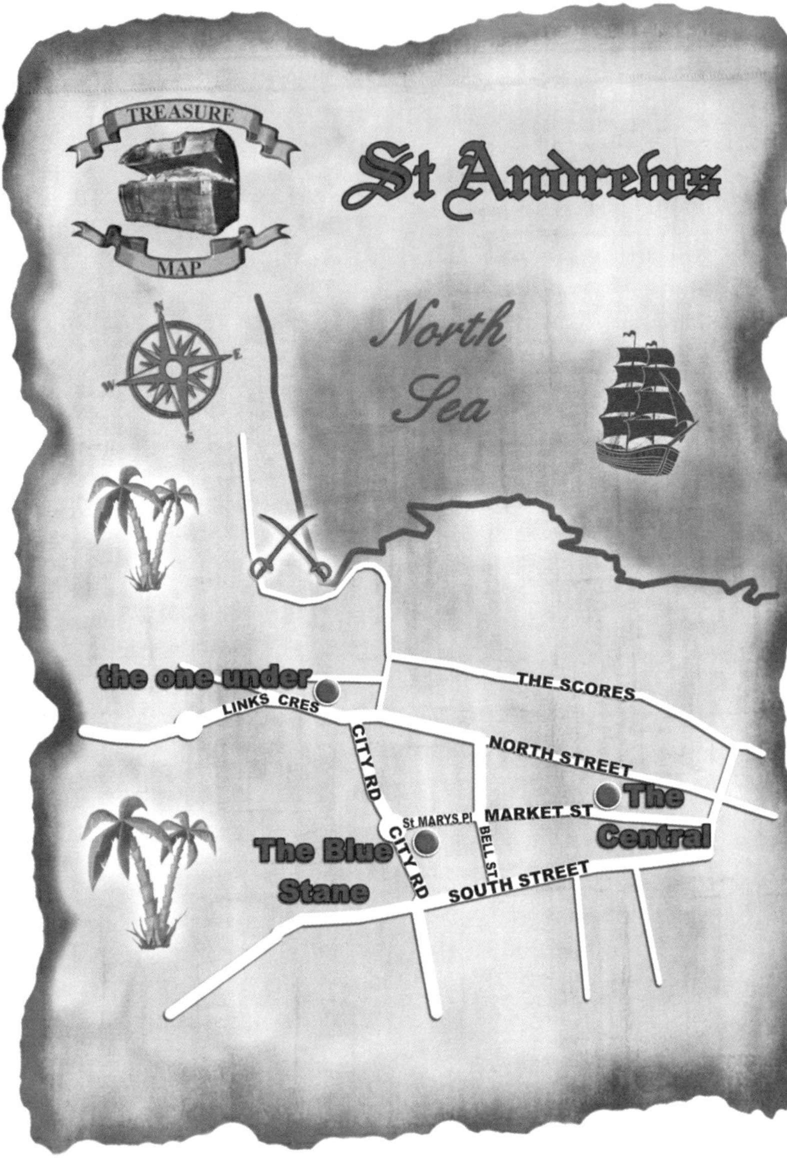

TREASURE
MAP
St Andrews
North Sea
N
E
W
S
the one under
LINKS CRES
THE SCORES
CITY RD
NORTH STREET
The Central
MARKET ST
St MARYS PL
BELL ST
The Blue Stane
CITY RD
SOUTH STREET

John: ***The journey.*** St. Andrews, home of Golf and Scotland's oldest University. One of the most famous places in the country. Royalty, and many wealthy and famous people have been educated there, so it stands to reason that they must have visited the beaches in the town and dropped a fortune during their drink and-drug filled orgies.

I learned on a previous wee overnight visit to the town that it is also famous for Proddies and Catholics fighting and killing each other; there are monuments to the dead all over the place, so old swords and weapons of torture must be there to be found.

But, as always, my first task was to get us there, by bus, as quickly as possible. During my search through the Traveline web site, the first thing I discovered is that it takes over two and a half hours on the bus from Buchanan Street. Worse was to follow when Citylink wouldn't let me book a seat in advance. It might have been my fault; at least that was Craig's opinion. Anyway, I came up with the idea of booking a seat on the bus to Dundee. I knew I could do this as I have done it before. Also, the journey is only one hour and forty minutes, and Dundee to St. Andrews looked pretty close on the map, so I reckoned it would be a quick journey over the Tay Bridge.

I checked and was happy to find out that it was only a half hour run, so adding the two bus journeys and the waiting time at Dundee, it still worked out a bit quicker than the direct route. Is that not amazing? The only problem was that, as Craig pointed out, my track record of organising buses, especially ones that have to join up, has sometimes lacked accuracy. I pointed out to him that a bus missed is just an opportunity to go somewhere else. He didn't see the funny side of that comment.

Our journey to St. Andrews was seamless. We got a number 6 into town, and even got a number 240 from George Square to the Bus Station. I had checked out this possibility on the Traveline web page. This saved us the uphill walk and also Craig's feet, which were louping. Mind you, he still complained that the stance the bus stopped at was a fair distance from where our Dundee bus was leaving from. There's no pleasing some folk.

There was a big queue for the M9 Aberdeen via Dundee coach, and we had to sit on two aisle seats. The couple who got the last pair of seats had jumped the queue in front of us. Craig was seething mad. The bus stopped at the Park and Ride just outside Perth and dozens of people got off to get another coach somewhere else. We managed to get seats together right at the front, so we had a great view of the last 30 minutes of the journey into Dundee.

Our next bus, the number 99 was waiting for us on stance four and we were on our way over the Tay Road Bridge in no time at all. It's a lovely run through Fife to St. Andrews, and the sun was out when we pulled into the bus station.

Craig had, as usual, been on the Google Earth page and had found what looked like a nice wee pub just across the road. So we crossed the road and went down a few stairs into *The Blue Stane.*

Craig: *Today's Beaches and Bars.* Today's trip to St Andrews was John's idea. I'm not a great fan of golf or golf courses. In fact, if you ask me, it is a waste of good building land. We could solve the entire housing crisis overnight if we just handed all of that underused land over to the developers. An added bonus would be an end to that boring patter in the pub every time there is a big tournament on the telly. It's like listening to a foreign language.

John on the other hand is besotted with the game. Every time we pass a half-way famous golf course, when we are out on one of our bus trips, he launches into some complicated story about the time he once played there. I have noticed that these stories usually end up with him in the clubhouse bar getting legless; so much for the health giving effects of a day out on the golf course.

Anyway, St Andrews is the widely accepted home of golf and John insisted that we visit it. I came up with the idea of telling him that there was no beach in St Andrews. I was banking on the fact that anytime he has ever visited the town to watch a tournament, like The Open, he never got much beyond the refreshment tent and had to watch the highlights on the television to find out what actually happened that day.

Before I got the chance to implement my plan John managed to scupper all my efforts. One dark night in *The Stoat Inn* he told me that he had heard that there was a great beach in the town. Apparently he had once been watching the film 'Chariots of Fire', and some know-all had told him that the beach all the athletes were skelping along in the title sequence was actually the beach right beside The Old Course in St Andrews.

It was bad enough that my best laid plan had gone agley, but I had the vague notion that the know-all who had blabbed was me.

I had compiled my usual in depth research the night before our trip, and things were not looking good. The pubs nearest to the beach, and therefore to The Old Course, looked to be a bit on the posh side. That really shouldn't have come as much of a surprise, in a town which seems to cater almost exclusively for rich American tourists.

However, while I was checking the position of the town's bus station I did notice a slightly less touristy pub, just a few yards down the road. It looked like the kind of place where a couple of thirsty travellers, who had spent a total of three and a half hours on buses that morning, might find a comfortable barstool, and a reasonably priced pint.

The Blue Stane is quite a quirky wee pub. It could be described as a semi-basement, being down a few steps from the main road.

It takes its name from a Pictish relic, said to have been used as the coronation stone for King Kenneth McAlpine. The relic, or Blue Stane, can be found in the churchyard, across the road from the pub.

I thought it was a friendly pub. The barmaid spotted us coming in and shouted over a cheery hello. As soon as we found a couple of barstools the customer sitting next to us started chatting away to us. I think he had just popped into *The Stane* while his wife was doing a bit of shopping.

The Blue Stane, St Andrews

We got into a light-hearted West Coast/East Coast competition, trying to outdo each other by naming the worst towns in our two areas. Our new drinking buddy, Stuart Kenny, won that contest. He said, "If you come to east, you really should to stop off in Bathgate, otherwise you won't believe a place like that exists."

John mentioned that his son, Campbell, who was over here on holiday from Australia, would be joining us for a beer. When he heard about this Australian connection Stuart told us that he had spent a lot of time over there. That led to the pair of them swapping stories of their adventures down under. These stories always seemed to involve beer, rugby and the number of lethal beasties out there just waiting to sink their fangs into unwary tourists.

When Campbell did arrive in the pub things got even worse. Stuart was wearing a rugby top belonging to the very Sidney club Campbell supports. Although they had never clapped eyes on each other they started chatting away like long lost friends.

Campbell and Stuart inThe Blue Stane

I was reduced to sipping my beer and looking out of the window, while rugby league, a sport even less interesting than golf, making it quite possibly the most boring sport invented by man, was discussed, dissected and generally boasted about.

In an effort to avoid being accidentally dragged into that conversation I started one of my own with the barmaid, Victoria McGrow. Like almost everyone else serving behind the bars of the pubs and hotels in St Andrews, Victoria is a university student.

I suppose that is a good thing, making university affordable to these young people, but it does also mean that there are very few really experienced bar staff in the town.

That might not matter to rich American tourists, drinking their top-of-the-range single malts, but, when you are asking a wee lassie, barely aged to be drinking herself, if she could recommend a good draught beer, you are going to be in trouble. Just for the record, I would like to point out that Victoria is a first class barmaid.

Usually, when we visit pubs there is a particular ritual we have to go through. I have to ask the person behind the bar if it would be all right if I take their picture for the book. The response to this request is almost always negative, but said in such a way as to suggest that they could be convinced otherwise.

John gives Campbell a few pointers

Things were different today. Victoria turned on her heel and ran out of the bar. This led us to believe that she was either painfully shy or a wanted criminal on the run from the law. I am pretty sure it was the first of these options, but John was unconvinced.

When we left *The Blue Stane* we headed for the beach, or at least that's where we headed after a short, but heated, discussion with John. Being a veteran of so many trips to St Andrews, John had insisted on taking charge of our navigation around the town.

A few minutes into one of his 'short cuts' I had to point out that there was very little chance of us finding the beach at the top of the hill we were climbing. Eventually we found ourselves standing on the road which runs along the side of the famous 18th fairway of the historic Old Course.

This of course meant that we had to stand and watch several groups of exceedingly untalented golfers hacking their way towards the final hole. It is hard enough watching professionals play golf, but some of these people were utterly hopeless.

I very nearly had an accident, laughing at one wee foreign woman who took a swing at her ball, missed and managed to knock her own hat off. I turned to share the moment with John and Campbell, but found they were not laughing along. Apparently golf is a very serious business, even when it is being played by people who have zero talent for it.

Rusack's Hotel sits next to the 18th fairway. Underneath the hotel we found our next port of call. From the outside *The One Under* bar looked to be an expensive place to visit. Unfortunately for us it lived up to its reputation once we got inside.

Having said that, it looked pretty ordinary on the inside; whatever the bar's owners are spending the profits from their vastly over-priced drinks on, it isn't on the décor of the place.

I mention the drink being expensive because I still can't believe what they charged us for the three standard sized bottles of Carlsberg lager we ordered. We were charged £10.65. I don't even like Carlsberg, and I certainly don't like drinking it out of a bottle; but we had little choice.

The young bloke who served us did put three glasses on the bar for us but, since they were just out of the dishwasher and were still burning hot, we left them sitting on the bar.

Incidentally, the reason for choosing Carlsberg was purely financial. It was all we were willing to part with in this pub.

Our barman, Caelen Barns, offered us some bottles of

Stella Artois but, since John had left his credit card at home, we declined. He mentioned that there was no draught beer in the place; he had no idea why this was the case, and didn't seem inclined to find out.

Caelen and Julia in
The One Under, St Andrews

He did provide us with a great laugh however when he tried to work out our change. I lost count of how often he had to go back to the till. What made this even funnier was he had to admit that he was studying Maths at university. John fell about laughing when he found this out.

Caelen, in his own defence, told us that they didn't use numbers in maths. I asked him if, at some time, between going to school at the age of five and entering one of Britain's greatest universities, he had never actually had reason to use numbers, but he either didn't hear me or he decided he had spent enough time talking to three cheapskates. Apparently a sense of humour is also not a requirement for entry into the maths department.

Julia, the other barperson, came over to help with the

change giving problem. She is from Livingston and is also studying at university. I asked her if *The One Under* was the kind of place that she and her pals would choose to socialise. She just laughed and said that she could barely afford to work there never mind have a drink.

Between them, Caelen and Julia managed to come up with the names of a few pubs which might suit us better. It's just a pity that they couldn't tell us before we shelled out all of that cash on the bottled beer.

As we left *The One Under* I was half expecting a uniformed doorman to be waiting outside for a tip. There wasn't one, of course; but let me tell you, if there had been, there would have been no cash changing hands.

The one thing I did quite like about this pub was its name. It is obviously a play on words. Being the bar below the main hotel, it is 'the one under. Also, in golfing terminology, 'one under' refers to being one under par, which is apparently a good thing, if you are a golfer.

However, to my mind, the name of this bar also sums up the experience of having a drink in the place. It is well under par in the value for money department.

Once we got to the beach we started unpacking our gear. Campbell decided the whole thing was far too embarrassing for him and he left to check on his car which was parked some distance away.

There were quite a few people about on the beach and I have to admit I could see his point. His dad and I had knocked back a few beers and were therefore unable to be embarrassed. Campbell, having his car with him, had only had a small, but very expensive, bottle of beer and felt well out of his comfort zone.

The odd thing was, although there were lots of people on the beach, not one person even looked in our direction while we were scanning the sand. Usually some nosey bugger will come over to ask us what we are doing. St Andrews folk must be too sophisticated, or stuck up, to talk to strangers on the beach, even ones who are doing odd, yet interesting things out there.

We found a few coins but nothing really exciting. Then the detector let out a really loud bleep. John, who had been eating his sandwiches, leapt into action, shovelling like a man possessed. He was more than a little angry when he dug up the silver foil which had been wrapped around my pieces.

While he had been busy, I had buried the foil in the sand. the strange thing was, we got another hit in the same spot, just a few moments later. I had to promise John that this wasn't another one of my attempts at humour before he would start digging again.

This time we did find something substantial. It was a metal spike about eight inches long. John was absolutely delighted, and unfortunately his imagination went into overdrive. He had been reading about religious martyrs and political conflicts in the history of St Andrews, so anything we found would no doubt have some dark history of its own. The spike we found must therefore, in his imagination, have something to do with torture. The man could keep his own personal psychiatrist gainfully employed.

The spike we found was quite obviously a tent peg. It was a fair age and would possibly have been used on a large canvas tent, possibly left behind after a Boy Scout camp.

We were joined by Campbell for the last quarter of an hour on the beach. I knew he couldn't resist a wee shot at detecting. I hate to admit it, but I would have been really annoyed if he had discovered something really important the first time he had ever tried using the machine. Fortunately for our reputations, such as they are, Campbell failed to uncover a major treasure trove.

At the end of a stint on the beach our usual tactic is to make full speed to the nearest boozer and end the day celebrating with liquid refreshment. That wouldn't work today as the nearest pub was out of our price bracket. Campbell came to the rescue by offering us a lift into the centre of town to search for a more reasonable establishment.

He dropped us off outside *The Central* in Market Street. It looked perfect for our purposes: old fashioned and without the slightest hint of golfing memorabilia.

Jamie and Raahael in The Central

I think the interior of the pub could be described as Victorian in its décor; unfortunately it was very up to the minute in its pricing. John ordered a pint of lager and a vodka and soda from our barman, Jamie Elliott. When he delivered the drinks to the bar top we were required to hand over £10.

John couldn't help himself and let slip a rude, but very descriptive word. Jamie didn't bat an eyelid, in fact he told us, "That's what most people say to me when they buy their first drink". We didn't like the prices, but the honesty was welcome.

My pint was pretty ordinary, but you couldn't say the same about John's vodka. The glass it came in was amazing. I have been in a few pubs in my time but I've never seen Waterford Crystal spirit glasses used in a public bar.

John was still going on about the price of the drink when

Rachel Reid, the barmaid, came over to see what all the commotion was about. Don't get me wrong, it was a friendly discussion, with John regaling the staff and any customers within earshot, with tales of the many pubs he had visited, which had all been cheaper than *The Central*.

Rachel is yet another student who works part-time to subsidise her studies. Given the price of the booze in this town I wouldn't be surprised if St Andrews is the only university in Scotland to have an entirely teetotal student body.

Before we left *The Central* I suggested to John that he could offset the cost of our last drink by nicking the crystal glass, but since we hadn't had very much to drink, due to us not being rich enough to afford it, he wasn't up to such bravery.

Apart from the jaw-dropping cost of a refreshment in the place, *The Central* is a really good bar. If I am lucky enough to inherit a fortune, or win big in the lottery, I might consider having a drink in there again if I make a return visit to St Andrews.

The journey back to the bus station was a bit longer than we thought, so we decided to break it with another visit to *The Blue Stane*. Although more expensive than most of the pubs we visit, *The Stane* is considerably cheaper than the other pubs we stopped in today.

It had been a bit of a strange day; we had spent more money than on a normal day out, while managing to have less to drink.

That is entirely wrong as far as we are concerned.

John: ***A review of the day.*** St. Andrews is everything you would expect from Scotland's oldest University Town which has Royals visiting it all the time. The pubs are outrageously expensive and the shops are all very fancy. There are no beggars hanging about and very few pound shops. It's not the sort of place where Craig and I fit in well. The place, especially the golf course area, is stinking of money. Maybe I'm just jealous, who knows.

Having had that moan, we had a great time in the town, bars and beach. It was made even better by my oldest son Campbell joining us for some of the time. He is over from Australia for my youngest son Gregor's wedding, and is staying for a few days with his wife Kelly, their two kids and her mother in a caravan in Burntisland. So he drove up to St. Andrews for a few hours to escape. He even had a shot of trying to find buried treasure, he said he should be a natural as he lives 'down under'. You can see where his humour comes from.

Our *Ace Garrett 150* came up trumps again, finding an amazing relic, which you will see in the photo below ties in with the sordid torturist religious history of the town. I've described it under the photograph.

Our journey home went without a hitch. We even managed to get a Number 10 bus from outside the bus station down to the Central Station, where we got the train back to EK. Craig's Irene was waiting to take us straight home. As I've said before, if she didn't pick us up at the station, we would be straight into *The Monty* for a wee nightcap, or two.

So ended another day on the beach: well one hour out of four ain't bad. St. Andrews is worth a visit if you're passing that way. It's nice to see how the other half live. One last point. Some of the youngsters we met in the bars, who are at University studying various degrees, seemed as thick as mince. I wonder how they will survive in the real world, which seems to be going down the tubes at the moment. Only time will tell.

Today' s treasure finds

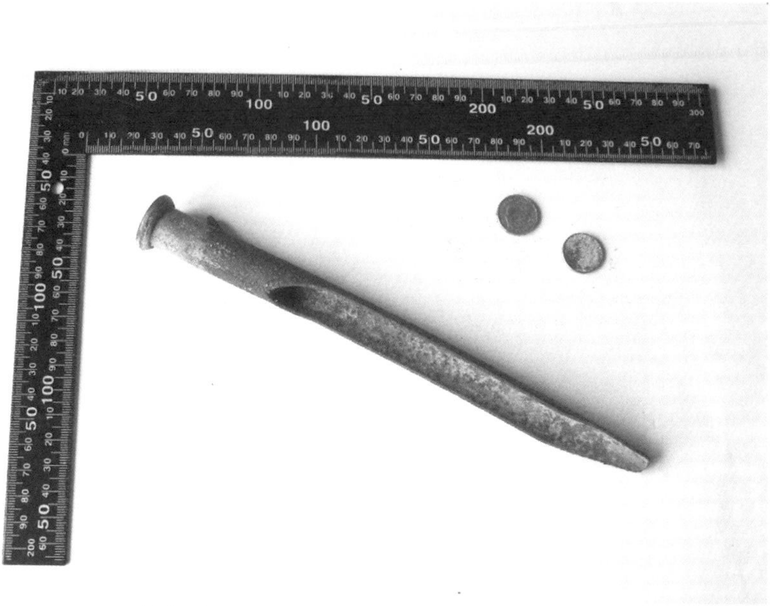

John's thoughts on today's finds;

At the beginning of today's story, I mentioned the religious battles and rampant torturing that was commonplace for a while in this neck of the woods. It is a fact that one of the most common methods of torture was to insert a red hot probe into the nether regions. You can see, if you study the spike closely, it even has a wee bit sticking out at the blunt end for a chord to be attached to pull out the prob after a confession has been forced from the poor prisoner.

I believe this could be a very valuable relic from St. Andrews' violent past.

Craig's thoughts on today’s finds;

I was really impressed with the tent spike we found. However the best ‘find’ of the day was the foil that I buried in the sand. John’s face was a picture when he found out what I had done.

How to get to St. Andrew' s (by bus from Buchanan Street)

The X24 will take you all the way. Mind you, it takes about two and a half hours.

On the other hand you can take the M9 Aberdeen bus which takes one hour and forty minutes and get off in Dundee Bus Station. From there take the No. 99 from stace 4. It takes about half an hour. The combined time is very slightly shorter than the direct bus, including the change over time in Dundee.

For a bit of variety, go directly and come back via Dundee.

Dumbarton-Beach?

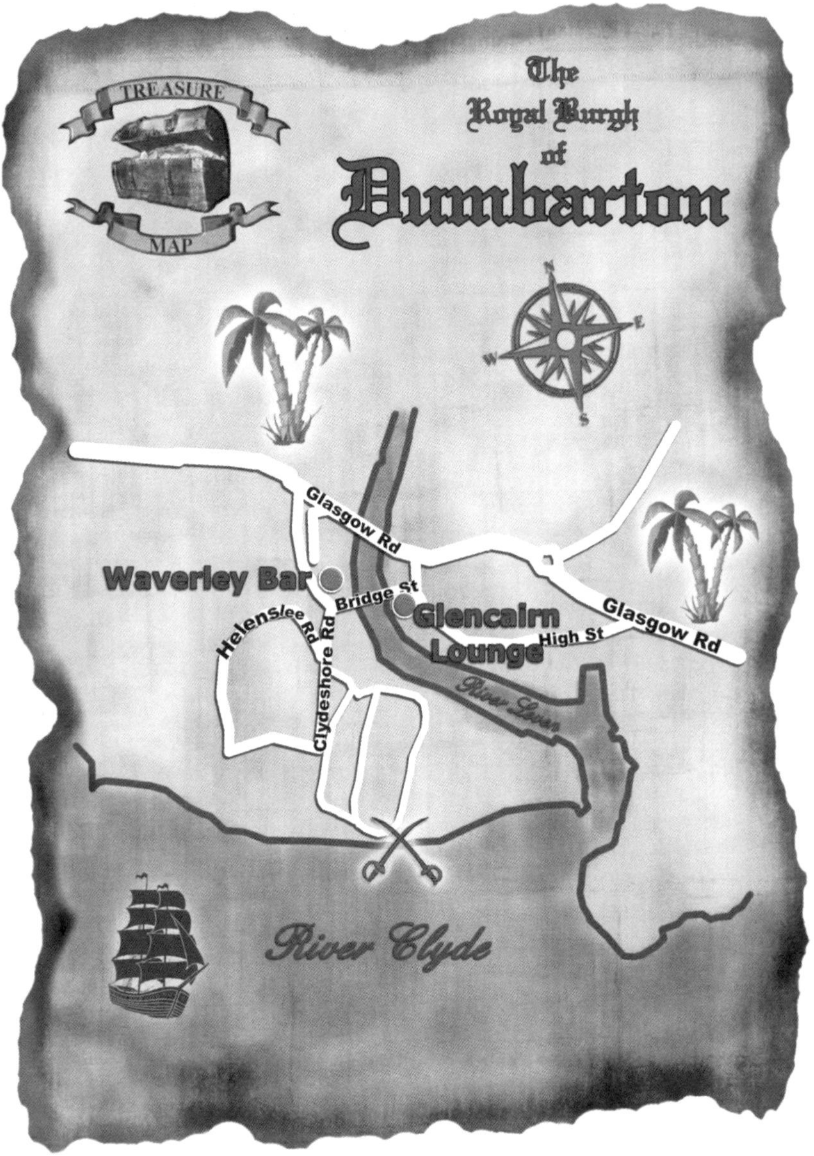

John; *The journey:* Why are we going to Dumbarton? I imagine anyone reading this chapter will be surprised by the venue. Apart from the Castle, most people reckon that it is not famous for beaches, bars, or anything else that we are looking for in this masterpiece. But they would be wrong.

Dumbarton is famous for many important things, whisky being one of them, but that is also not the reason we are here. As you all know, I am a man of the Clyde, and a great lover of Scotland's most beautiful coastal town, Rothesay, which, by the way, is no more than a few miles from today's beach.

In the 50s, up until the end of the 60s, if you stood on Rothesay Pier, as I did, especially between 9.00am and 11.00am on any morning of the week, you would see many of the great pleasure steamers of that era ploughing up and down the Clyde, almost all of them stopping at Rothesay. Now, you may not know this, but many of them were built in one of the world's greatest shipyards: Denny's of Dumbarton.

Among the hundreds built there were many Clyde favourites: *The Duchess of Montrose, The Loch Fyne, The Queen Mary, The Caledonia* (a favourite of mine), *The Queen Alexandria,* which became the famous three red-and-black-funnelled *Saint Columba,* and the world's first commercial Turbine Steamer, *The King Edward*. The names and my memories of these classic ships come back to me, and I know they will to you as well.

There were many more world-famous ships built at Denny's, including the completion and launching of *The Cutty Sark*, but I am more interested in local ships.

Now, with that much tonnage of shipping hammering up and down the Clyde, some built in other great shipyards, it stands to reason that there must be an amazing amount of interesting flanges and other nautical things lying buried in the local beach.

Another tiny, and unimportant detail is that our editor and friend Ian Baillie lives in the area, and was keen that we would cover one of his local beaches. Now Ian does all the editing for nothing, so this was another reason, to honour Ian!

As always, or most times, we want to take the bus. But today, as we were meeting Ian, who was joining us for the day, we left it to him to organise where wc would meet. He e-mailed to tell us to meet us at Dalreoch train station in Dumbarton. So we were forced to go by rail!

We were a bit concerned because our train was leaving from Queen Street, which was in in the middle of being dug up for improvements. I picked up Craig at ten sharp, to give us plenty of time to get into Glasgow. Our journey on the old number 18 was a breeze, and we arrived at Queen Street just before eleven. The train was leaving at 11.32am. With over half an hour to kill, there was only one thing to do, have a pint. So we did.

The bars in the station were all closed due to the renovations going on, so the closest was one of the bars we hate most, Wetherspoons, which is just outside the station, so in we went.

To be honest, I've been in one or two of their pubs, and they are not too bad, but this one is a really dark and depressing place. To be fair, the beer was ok, so we had our pint and headed for the train.

It was a lovely run down to Dumbarton, and with the bus pass you get a fair discount, which helps. Ian was waiting for us on the platform, and was excited and keen for us to visit one of his local pubs, *The Waverley,* which is owned by a friend of his, the Heart of Midlothian legend Drew Busby.

Now I am old enough to have seen Drew playing, and he was a great player. Ian had mentioned knowing him many times recently, and this was the main reason for coming to Dumbarton. It certainly wasn't for the beach, which Craig claimed didn't exist, and he said he had spent hours on '*Google Beach View*'!! Remember, Ian does our editing for nothing, apart from the odd drink, so I would have gone to a children's sand pit if he had asked!

Ian took us out of the station, over the main Dumbarton to Helensburgh Road, and down a wee street to the legendary *Waverley Pub,* with the legendary owner. It was shut!

It's hard to put in writing Craig's comments. Hard because Ian, or any normal person would edit them out. Needless to say his feet were louping, and again, the pub was shut. Ian tried to recover the situation by telling us that just round the corner and over the bridge which crosses The River Leven, there was a brilliant pub called *The Glencairn.* In we went. As usual I will let Craig carry on now with our story of our day in Dumbarton.

Craig: *Today's Beaches and Bars.* Since we were heading to Dumbarton, a place I know next to nothing about, I thought I had better have a wee look at the history of the place.

The town of Dumbarton was once known for shipbuilding but the last of the big yards, William Denny and Brothers closed its gates for the final time in 1963.

The world famous tea clipper, the Cutty Sark, was built in another of Dumbarton's yards, Scott & Linton.

Dumbarton Castle has had some very famous visitors in the past. William Wallace paid a surprise visit to the castle once, but wasn't too impressed. The problem was, his visit had been planned by English troops belonging to Edward the 1st of England. Wallace was held in the castle before being taken down to London for trial and execution.

The castle also has a connection with Mary Queen of Scots. If memory serves, that ended badly as well.

When people talk about Scotland's most famous beaches, few, if any, are likely to mention the golden sands of Dumbarton. There is a reason for that. Dumbarton has always been associated with heavy industry and is not seen as a resort town.

I would suggest that one of the main reasons for not packing your bags, buying the weans buckets and spades and heading for a beach holiday in Dumbarton is the fact that the town isn't actually on the coast. The town of Dumbarton sits on the banks of the River Clyde. I accept that it is a tidal stretch of river, but riverside is not beach front.

I had, as I've said, checked out our destination on my computer. No matter how hard I tried I could find no sign of sand dunes, beach huts or deckchair hire stalls. The chances of finding a decent beach bar definitely looked remote.

I think, from what I've just said, you will get the impression that choosing Dumbarton for today's destination was not my idea; and you would be correct. The only good thing about choosing this place was, when everything went catastrophically wrong, I wouldn't be catching any of the blame.

When we stepped off the train at Dalreoch Station in Dumbarton I noticed that we were the only passengers to do so. We were meeting Ian Baillie, our editor and mastermind behind this particular trip, on the platform and I felt that I just had to mention the total lack of holidaymakers. Where were all the happy families excitedly heading for the town's beaches? I asked him. Surely on such a warm day there should be hordes of sun-seekers, carrying deck chairs and beach brollies, charging off the train in an effort to bag the best spot on the beach.

I'm fairly certain that he detected a sarcastic tone to my questions, but he just laughed and suggested that we head to the nearest pub for a wee refreshment. This was a plan which very definitely got my vote, so we made our way down West Bridgend to *The Waverley.*

I had checked out this pub online and it looked quite promising. It is the nearest pub to the River Clyde and therefore, presumably, Dumbarton beach front.

It had the look of a traditional village pub about it. Unfortunately it also had the look of a pub which had failed to open for business. I said that this could be an omen for the rest of the trip, but Ian said that the pub on the other side of the bridge would definitely be open.

The Glencairn Lounge, on Bridge Street, was another traditional-looking pub and since we actually saw someone coming out of its front door we were fairly certain that it was open for business.

Judging by its exterior I expected to find a basic, run-of-the-mill working class pub inside. As soon as we pushed open the door I knew that I had got it wrong. There was carpet on the floor, and not just a wee bit; we are talking wall to wall.

That would usually be enough to have us turning on our heels and looking elsewhere for a refreshment. But, given the fact that we knew that the nearest was securely locked up, we decided to persevere.

The Glencairn Lounge was very modern, to our old eyes at least, but the big shock came when I noticed the tables. Obviously there is nothing wrong with a pub having tables about the place, but, these tables had menus and condiments on them. Things were looking bleak, from an old codger's perspective anyway.

Having wall-to-wall carpeting and selling food are two of the three things most likely to put off the mature drinking gentleman. All we needed was for a bus load of school kids to descend on the pub for lunch and we would have the treble.

In an attempt to get as far away as possible from the catering area of the pub we found some stools over at the bar, just around the corner.

It didn't look like we would be staying too long in this pub but we couldn't leave without having at least one drink.

I'm really glad that we did because I completely changed my mind about the place within a very short period of time.

Yvonne Armstrong, our barmaid, made us feel very welcome. In fact she just about made my day when she laughed out loud after hearing, from John, that we were looking for Dumbarton beach.

Yvonne is from Aberdeen and has only moved down to Dumbarton quite recently. In fact she has only been working in *the*

Glencairn for a few weeks. Ian took some comfort from that, arguing that that she hadn't been there long enough to know about all the local facilities. I'm fairly certain that he had his fingers crossed when he came out with this theory.

After chatting about the various Aberdeen pubs we had all visited, Yvonne managed to have a word with her boss, Carolyn Murray.

As soon as she heard from Yvonne that we were looking for the beach, Carolyn came over to check that she had heard properly. I really think she thought we were winding her up. Once again John had to get some of our books out to prove we were on the level.

Yvonne Armstrong & Carolyn Murray

She was very interested in the books and asked us what our favourite pub was. We are quite used to this question and, as we can't agree on the subject, we have a short list of some of the best we have come across on our seven year journey around Scotland.

It is when we are asked about the worst ones we have seen

that we are more in agreement. I mentioned the name of a certain pub in Aberdeen and Yvonne immediately agreed with our judgement. We compared our experiences in said pub and had a really good laugh.

However, when I suggested that *The Central Bar* in Renton could be a good candidate for the crappiest pub in the country I thought Carolyn was objecting. Actually I had misheard her.

I thought she said that her husband, Tommy, owned *The Central*. That led to a lot of back-tracking and a fair amount of grovelling, on my part. I even tried to stop John from showing her the chapter in the book about that pub. It has a really scary looking picture of the outside of the pub and a fairly critical review of just about everything on the inside.

Instead of going into a huff Carolyn actually bought the three of us a drink. I thought that was a strange reaction, but John explained that Carolyn's husband hadn't owned the pub, he had only worked there for a while.

It was about this time that Tommy himself walked into the bar. The girls were quick to fill him in on our story. Once again there was a great deal of laughing when he heard what we were up to. Apparently it isn't every day that beachcombers turn up in his pub.

We chatted for a while about pubs in the area and of course someone mentioned *The Central*. Thankfully, Tommy agreed that it was in a pretty poor state, but pointed out that it had become quite famous in recent years. Because it hasn't changed much in the last century or so, film companies are keen to use it as a backdrop when filming historical dramas.

I mentioned to Tommy that I had mistakenly thought he had been the owner of *The Central* and after having a good laugh at that idea he told us a few tales of his time behind the bar up in Renton.

It has a bit of a reputation as a tough pub where the staff take no prisoners. Tommy said that a customer came into the bar one night and asked for a bottle of Beck's. The barmaid, a bit of a rough diamond, replied, "Dae ye think this is a f....n Bistro?"

One of the reasons we were in Dumbarton was because Ian wanted us to see *The Waverley* pub. It is owned by somcone he knows. Drew Busby is a well-known former Hearts player and Ian has been a Hearts fan since he was a boy.

He is also a fan of junior side Vale of Leven which, given how unsuccessful they are, makes him almost unique. He must therefore have thought it was his birthday when Tommy revealed that he had once played for the Vale.

Tommy and two bar flys

Usually when fans and players get together they end up reminiscing about past club glories. But since it is Vale of Leven we are talking about, those kind of stories are a bit thin on the ground. However, Tommy did tell us a good story about his early days in junior football.

He played his first game at the age of 17 and managed to score two goals to win the game. The win was so unexpected that the after match drink went on late into the night. Tommy was still wandering around the clubhouse in his football strip at ten o'clock. I think he got into quite a bit of trouble when he eventually got back home that night.

The drink was certainly flowing in *The Glencairn,* especially when Tommy insisted on buying yet another round. John, not to be outdone reciprocated. I was beginning to think that the metal detector would be staying safely in its bag for the rest of the day. Since I was quite sure that there was no beach to be searched, this prospect didn't bother me one little bit.

Ian was still insisting that he knew exactly where we could find a good piece of beach that would suit our purposes. After much thought Tommy proclaimed that he did in fact know a bit of the river bank that had a sandy stretch on it.

The selling point of his 'beach' was its location; it was not that far around the corner from the pub. I still wasn't convinced but I felt I had to go along with John and Ian on their mission to find Dumbarton's hidden beach paradise, although the prospect of spending the rest of the day exactly where I was sitting was very tempting.

It quickly became clear that even if it existed the beach was not 'just around the corner'. What was around the corner was Levengrove Park. At any other time I would have been quite happy to have a wander through the park but, I was under a lot of pressure at that particular moment.

My foot was giving me a bit of pain and I didn't know how much longer I could keep walking. I was also under another kind of pressure. Due to all of the handshaking, backslapping and laughter as we were getting ready to leave *The Glencairn*, I had neglected to visit the gents before leaving the pub. It was a rookie mistake and it could've had disastrous consequences.

Ian didn't help my predicament by insisting on a detour as we crossed the park. He wanted to show us a stone plaque which had been laid to mark the burial site of some of the remains of Scotland's greatest king: Robert the Bruce.

It would seem that after his death, from leprosy, the king's body was dismembered. His heart was removed and eventually buried in Melrose Abbey, the body was interred in Dunfermline Abbey and his internal organs, or viscera, were buried in the grave which can now be found in Levengrove Park.

I'm all for a bit of history but the timing of this lesson was a bit off. I hadn't had my lunch at that point and all the talk of ripping out intestines was doing little to help my appetite.

Ian and John try to chisel a hole in the 'sand'

After a hard slog across the park we eventually reached the river bank. John and Ian were delighted; they had found their beach. Now I don't think that I'm particularly hard to please but, in my opinion, this patch of barren ground was no beach. I've knocked more sand out of my shoes after a short stroll along Ayr beach than there was on this piece of wasteland. Had we been searching for fag ends and sweetie wrappers we would have found rich pickings.

Like a true optimist, I tried to make the best of it and

proceeded to scan the tip we were standing in. I got a few rogue signals but, as expected, found precisely hee-haw.

That was probably just as well as digging through the sand might have proved difficult; it was more hard packed dirt than sand really. Besides, there was no telling what we might have dug up in the lower reaches of the River Clyde. It did seem like the ideal spot for an up-and-coming junkie to ply his trade of an evening.

By way of deflecting the blame for landing us in this rubbish dump, John pointed over to Dumbarton Rock and said that at least we had a great view of the castle. I countered this by telling him that the people up in the castle had a great view of three daft auld buggers staggering around a midden.

Eventually my two companions had to admit that we were not going to find anything of interest and that it was time to move on.

Moving on in this instance meant heading for the nearest pub, but there was some debate as to which one that was. I was in favour of a return to *the Glencairn* Lounge, while Ian wanted to try *The Waverley* again. He thought that it probably didn't open before lunchtime on mid-week days but, by this time it would likely be quite busy. John had the casting vote and opted for *The Waverley*. I had to go along with the decision but it occurred to me that the way my day had been going so far, it was quite likely that we would find the place boarded up and a for sale sign stuck on the front door.

Thankfully *The Waverley* was open, but only just by the look of it; we were the first customers. It is a fair sized bar, a bit modern, but comfortable.

Our barmaid was Maria McGee and she seemed genuinely glad to see us. We don't get that a lot so we knew we had landed lucky. Once we got talking it was obvious that Maria was up for a laugh. She certainly got one when we told her that we had been down the beach looking for treasure.

Maria McGee, The Waverley

She has worked in The Waverley for over 30 years, and she told us that we were the first people she had ever met who had managed to find a beach in Dumbarton. I think she even suggested that we alert the local newspapers, just in case someone had lost it and was looking to get it back.

According to Maria, *The Waverley* gets a good cross-section of punters. Unlike some pubs, the older guys get on with the younger set, and there is rarely any trouble in the place.

Just to prove the point, a young guy wandered into the bar and nodded to us in the passing. His name was Danny and we chatted to him for a while. He agreed with Maria about the friendliness and character of the pub.

I thought I had misheard him when he ordered his first drink and had to ask him what he had said. He was happy to tell me that his preferred tipple was called two and one. We were still scratching our heads at this when Maria plonked down two glasses of vodka and a can of coke. I had to ask. It was all quite logical when he explained. He uses one can of coke for two drinks. To be sure that he gets an equal amount of Coke in his vodka every time, he fills his glasses side-by-side.

Danny and his two and one

When this kind of thinking starts to make sense, you know that either you have been drinking all day or that you are a lost cause.

We didn't have a lot of time left before we needed to catch our train back into Glasgow, but we made the most of it.

The drink was good and the patter was even better. Who cares if the day had been a total waste of time?

A few days after the trip I did find a strip of sand further down the river. I had been checking satellite pictures of the area on my computer. I'm thinking of sending a picture of it to Ian, to prove that he had been right all along.

The only problem with this beach is that it is next to a water treatment plant and the locals seem to be using the golden sands as the final resting place of several old mattresses and a lot of un-bagged household waste. Rich pickings indeed!

John: ***A review of the day.*** We found nothing! I think Craig did not want to find anything as he at first said there was no beach, then when we found a wee bit of sand, he said it was crap. I have a feeling he had the machine turned off when he was using it. He knows how to hold a grudge. I thought the beach, small though it was, was lovely.

The sun shone all day, and we had a fabulous view of the rock and the river. Granted, the beach itself was small, but big enough for a couple of old codgers like us to spend a happy hour on.

Before we went down to the beach, we had had a right few in *The Glencairn*, which is one of the best pubs I have had the pleasure of visiting. It had things Craig and I don't like: carpets, and big restaurant, which was full, and children in the restaurant. But even with all that, the pub was made by the girls behind the bar and Tommy, the owner.

On the way back from our fruitless visit to the beach, Craig and I wanted to go back to *The Glencairn*, but Ian was desperate for us to meet Drew. So we went up to see if *The Waverley* was open-it was- and Ian was delighted. In we went. Ian's first words to the barmaid were 'is Drew in?'. 'No', said the barmaid. 'Will he be in this afternoon', Ian cried desperately. 'No' said the barmaid. Ian took a tanking from Craig. 'Editor, you call yourself" Craig roared. 'You couldn't edit the Dandy'. Craig's instant put-downs can sometimes be a bit crap!

We had a great time in *The Waverley.* Maria McGee, the barmaid of over 30 years, was brilliant company and kept us laughing at her stories for about half a dozen pints.

At about six o'clock we headed back to the station. On the way Ian got a text from his wife wondering where the hell he was. That's the watered-down version. We left him to his excuses and jumped on the Glasgow train wondering if we had just lost our editor.

The journey home was uneventful, except for Craig moaning about the crap beach and the no star football player. I had a great day and got home still a wee bit tipsy. Kate said I was pissed.

John's thoughts on today's finds;

I told Craig it was not the finding, but the hunting that was important. I also mentioned that we may have had more success if he had shown more enthusiasm and turned the damned thing on. Ah well, you can't win every day.

Craig's thoughts on today's finds;

I think they were lucky to find any sand, never mind any artefacts.

How to get to Dumbarton (by bus from Buchanan Street)

From Buchanan Street get a 240 or X36 and get off down on Argyle Street. Unless you have to go into the bus Station just make your way along Argyle Street past the Radisson Hotel and pick up a 1A going to Balloch or a 1B going to Helensburgh. It takes about an hour. There are buses regularly.

You can if you want take the train, but it takes money. Train leaves from Queen Street and is only half an hour.

Trip to the top

(Thurso, Aberdeen, Montrose, Carnoustie)

John; ***The Planning:*** In our last book (The Auldest Boozers in Toon), we finished with a trip as far north as Mallaig, with overnight stops on the way. Craig did not think we had gone far enough north. He demanded that for once we go all the way to the top, without the women (they had come with us in the last book).

For the last six books Craig has complained that we have done nothing for the people of the far North. I asked him what they had ever done for us. 'That's not the point', was his reply, 'we must go to the very North of Scotland'.

Once we agreed that the trip should be carried out, we both thought that apart from Thurso, which is at the very top of Scotland, we should visit Skye, for obvious reasons!

Author's note: Most people think that John o' Groats is the most northerly point. Our loyal readers will know, of course, that we must go to the most northerly point that has a few pubs in it- thus Thurso got the nod.

Getting back to Skye. Have you ever tried to book accommodation there in the summer! It's cheaper to go to Tenerife for a week. Which, to be honest, is not a bad idea. After we got over the shock of the prices, or Craig to be more precise, we decided to go somewhere else. The problem is that once you get to Thurso, which is a hell of a way away, everywhere else is a hell of a way from Thurso.

We decided that since we must get back to Inverness first of all, the easiest places to visit would be in the East Coast, and since we had not covered that area as much as the West, we thought it was only fair on the Easterners that we give them a visit (is Easterners a real word)?

It was decided that this was going to be a three night trip, a first for us. Since Craig refused to sleep with me, story of my life really, it would be an expensive trip. Each night would have to be two single rooms. Craig was adamant he had his own room.

After much planning and changing, we decided we would head for Aberdeen first, then Montrose, and lastly Carnoustie. We felt that was giving the East a good coverage. I was charged with organising the accommodation and buses. What could go wrong!

To be fair, it was not that difficult to get the accommodation we wanted at a reasonable price. I thought Aberdeen would be a nightmare, but it turned out that a Saturday night in the B & Bs is not as busy as midweek, when the oil workers from all over Scotland descend on the place for their week's work. The truth is that Aberdeen in general is not as busy now as it used to be, due to the oil crisis.

Before I was allowed to confirm the bookings, Craig insisted we go on to the web and check out the reviews of each B & B. I told him I had no idea how to do that sort of thing. So Craig did the checking, and once I got his approval, I booked all three nights on the phone. If the people sounded nice, that was fine with me.

The good thing is that if any of them are crap, I can blame him for not checking the reviews properly.

Once all the three B & Bs were booked, I set about booking us on all the buses we would need. I even booked us on two buses for most of the major journeys in case we missed the first one. Talk about belt and braces, I was beginning to feel this four day, three night trip might work. Who am I kidding. We will probably end up in Partick!

Our trip was to be from Friday to Monday, it was the end of August and we hoped the weather might be reasonable. Up until now the summer had been crap. At last, the Friday morning arrived and we were off for our adventure to Teuchter land.

Thurso

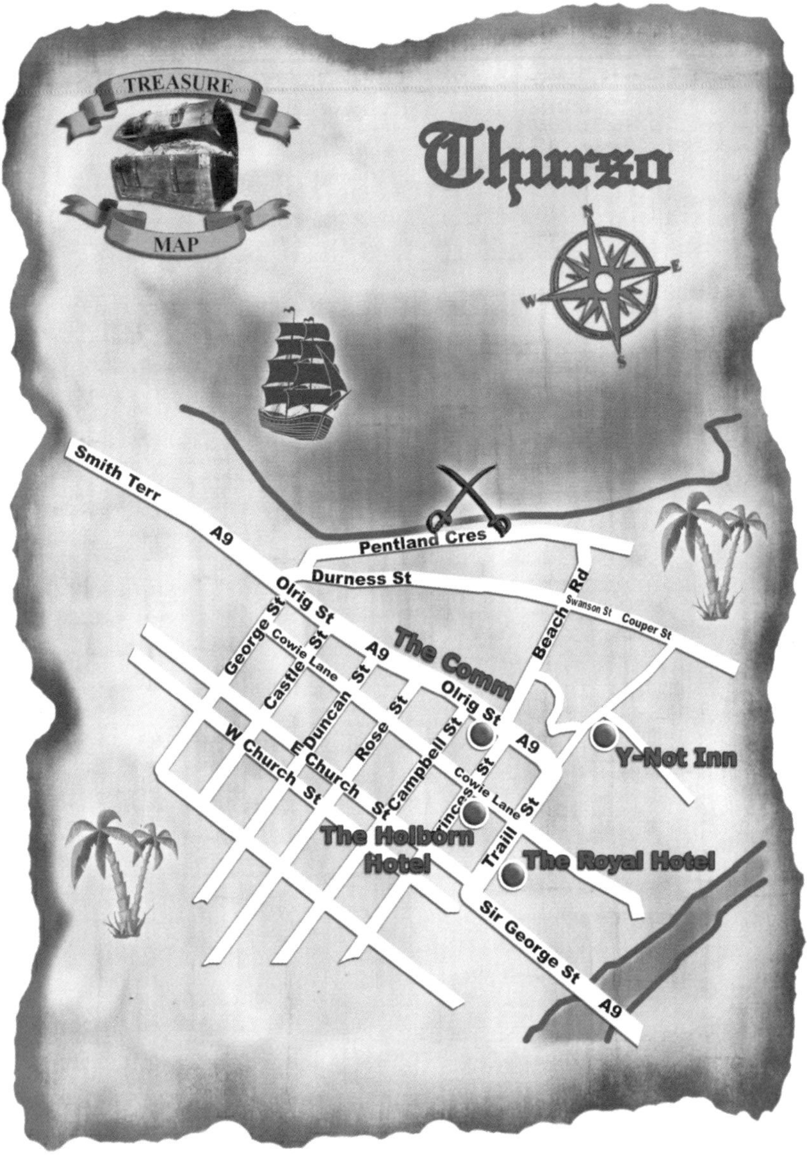
TREASURE
MAP
Thurso
N
E
W
S
Smith Terr
A9
Pentland Cres
Durness St
Olrig St
George St
Cowie Lane
Castle St
A9
Duncan St
The Comm
Beach Rd
Swanson St
Couper St
Rose St
Olrig St
Campbell St
A9
W Church St
E Church St
Princess St
Cowie Lane
Y-Not Inn
Traill St
The Holborn Hotel
The Royal Hotel
Sir George St
A9

John: ***The journey.*** Today was going to be a hell of a long one. Craig had insisted that we get the 7.30am (in the morning) bus, so that we would get to Thurso at 3.15pm. His point was that we would then have plenty of time to do our metal detecting, have something to eat, and still get pissed before going to our separate rooms. This meant leaving EK at the back of six. Neither of the girls could run us into Glasgow. My Kate was away in Kilwinning looking after her sister who had just gone through a wee procedure involving things I know nothing about. I reckon Craig's Irene just couldn't be arsed!

I played safe and booked us on the 9.00am Gold Bus as well, just in case we missed the early morning one. The later bus would still get us to Thurso by five thirty. I tried to explain that it never gets dark up there in the summer, so we would still have time to do our detecting and have a good bevy. There was no arguing with him, it was the seven thirty bus out of Glasgow.

So, as the wife was away, I had to pack my own bag. What would I take? After much thought, I packed a couple of extra pairs of socks, undies and shirts, as well as some toiletries. I had to pack my bags and make my pieces the night before as I would have to be up at about half five, or would I?

After a bit of thought the night before our journey, Craig said he was worried at the very early start and the walking up from George Square to the bus station before his joints had loosened up, so he talked me into booking a taxi. A Kelvin Cab picked us up at 6.30am, and in no time at all we were at the bus station in Buchanan Street.

As usual, Craig got into a mood when people from abroad, who have no concept on the techniques of queueing, jumped in in front of us. Worse was to follow when a couple of youngsters did the same. Young people nowadays don't have the same respect for us oldies that we used to have for our elders. I tried to point out to him that there only about 20 or so people wanting on the bus. 'That's not the point' he shouted, so the culprits would hear him. I said I agreed to get him to settle down.

Soon we were on our way on the G9 Gold Bus service to Inverness, one of the nicest journeys in Scotland. It felt like a new bus, and thankfully was a single decker, so it was comfortable. The new double-deckers they have introduced have very wide seats, that supposedly transform into beds. The beds must be bloody hard!

We had a laugh just after the bus left the station. A wasp must have got locked in the bus and was annoying a wee woman who started attacking it with her walking stick. She nearly had the window in with her swiping. The wasp was never seen again.

When we were going through Aviemore, an amazing thing happened. I got a call on my mobile from Hotpoint to tell me that they were coming on the 6th of September to fix our tumble drier. We had bought it almost a year ago, and it turned out to be one of these ones that bursts into flames with no warning. They had told us only to use it if you were in the house. So if it goes on fire, you go up in flames with the machine. The wife has never used the thing, and we were beginning to give up on ever tumbling anything. So there you go. All's well that ends well. That's if the bastards turn up.

Aviemore was busy. There was a Harley Davidson show on in the town, and the streets were alive with the bikes roaring about making a hell of a racket. It sounded brilliant. They are expecting about 5000 bikes. Craig said he still harbours the hope of owning a motor bike in the future. I told him that the roads are bad enough without him dottering about on a motor bike, and I doubted if there's a cow big enough to make a leather jacket to fit him. He was not amused.

About half an hour later we pulled into the bus station in Inverness. That was the journey half completed. We had about an hour to kill before our Thurso bus, so I talked Craig into going to my favourite pub in Inverness, *The Market Bar,* for a quick one. It's not the most glamorous bar in the city, and certainly not the prettiest, but the staff are brilliant, and the regulars are crazy. A perfect combination. The girls behind the bar, Mel and Shirley were on duty and remembered us. Shirley has worked in the bar for about 20 years, and has seen no changes to the bar, toilets or customers in that time! As always, we had a great time and soon were saying our goodbyes and heading back to the station to catch the X99 Thurso service.

At the station, we had a problem with the bay numbers and nearly missed the bus. I'm sure Craig will fill you in in more detail about how this near disaster came about, and whose fault it was.

Our X99 left, with us just on it, and we had a lovely journey to the very top of Scotland. On the way, the bus pulled in for a few minutes in Dunbeath. This is the birthplace of another great humorous Scottish author, Neil Munro.

It is an amazing coincidence that Neil Munro (under the pen name of Hugh Foulis) wrote the tales of Para Handy, who captained a Puffer called the Vital Spark, which steamed around Scotland, stopping off at wee ports all round the country, and ending up having a good bevy wherever he stopped. We do the exact thing, only we use the bus. Makes me feel proud.

If you are travelling to Orkney via Gill's Ferry Terminus, this is where you change buses. Thought I would let you know this just in case you are ever going by bus to these islands.

We arrived in Thurso on schedule, and had only a few yards' walk to our Hotel, *The Royal*, to start our adventure in the North.

I'll let Craig take it from here and tell you all about our excesses.

Craig: ***The day's Beaches and Bars.*** We were planning the final stages of our latest book while enjoying some liquid refreshment in our homemade pub, when the idea for this chapter was first proposed. Looking back on it, perhaps we should have approached it in a more professional, and sober, fashion.

Our first plan was to include islands like Skye and Mull in our round Scotland adventure. The thinking behind that was quite simple; being islands they had to have some reasonable beaches for us to visit.

What we hadn't initially factored in was cost. On our budget we could probably just about manage one night on Skye before the kitty purse was empty.

After a lot of debate, and quite a few beers, we decided to do the exact opposite of that first proposal. Instead of heading North and West we would be travelling North and East.

I'm fairly sure that it was my idea to include Thurso on our itinerary. John has been there before, so I can't really see him wanting to go back there, not voluntarily anyway!

Since I had managed to get my first choice accepted, I left the choosing of the other destinations to John. Time would tell if that had been a smart move or not. Due to a chronic lack of imagination on John's part, I got to choose the last destination as well.

Having visited Sandhead, down on the Mull of Galloway, the most southerly point in Scotland, it was very important to me that we should pay a visit to the most northerly point as well.

John insisted that we should take in Aberdeen beach, mainly because he wanted to visit our favourite pub in that city. Also on his list was the town of Montrose, for reasons he never fully explained. That left us with one slot still to fill and, after a lot of searching, I came up with the famous golfing town of Carnoustie.

Although not technically on our stayover list, we planned to stop over in Inverness for an hour before resuming our journey north. I would have been happy enough to just nip into a wee café to kill the time between buses, but John would have none of that.

He was determined to revisit one of our favourite pubs in Inverness: *The Market Bar*. Once I had worked out that it wasn't too far away from the bus station, I agreed that we should nip round there for a quick pint.

If you don't already know where *The Market Bar* is, it can be very difficult to find. We had to enlist the services of a local guide the first couple of times we visited it. Our guide, better known as John's brother Robert, had taken us there to show us one of the oldest pubs in the city.

The Market Bar Inverness

It is to be found up a close leading off Church Street. Completely by accident we found that it can also be located by using one of the exits of the Victorian Market, though it is a bit like finding your way through a maze.

As I've said we have been in this pub a few times before, but somehow we are always a bit surprised when we actually find it. We introduced ourselves to the barmaid, Shirley, whom we had not seen before on our visits. Shirley was convinced that we must have been trying to avoid her as she had been working there for 23 years.

Over a beer we told her about our books and the penny

dropped. She said that the staff and customers had enjoyed one of the stories about the pub in one of our earlier books. It concerned one of the pub's customers who did not want to give us his name. He was 'outed' by another customer who called out his name as he was leaving the pub.

Mel and Shirley, The Market Bar, Inverness

Before leaving we met up with Mel, the other barmaid. We had talked to her the last time we had been in the place. I had just finished my pint when one of the girls, I will not reveal which one, said, "Look there's Harry coming in". Of course I had to ask "Who's Harry?" Only to be told that he was the guy who didn't want us to put his name in our book.

Back at the bus station John got his travel document file out to check our arrangements. I was suitably impressed. He confidently announced that our bus up to Thurso would be leaving from stance three in ten minutes.

By my reckoning we had been standing patiently waiting for about eight minutes before it occurred to me that, just maybe my friend, the travel mastermind, had once again arsed things up.

I asked him if he was absolutely sure we were at the right stance. My concern was raised when I heard the bus behind us start up. On the side of it, in two foot high letters it said, 'TO THE NORTH'. I took that as a clue and insisted that he go round and check.

Seconds later he was shouting and waving his wee arms about like a badly regulated windmill. We were indeed standing at the wrong stance.

At least the driver enjoyed the show; two old guys tripping over their bags and shouting a mixture of threats and encouragement at each other. To avoid listening to further criticism John pretended to be asleep for most of the journey up to Thurso.

It had been quite a journey and as usual we thanked the driver as we got off the bus. John asked him if we would catch our bus back down from the same stop. The driver said that was right, and added that not only would it be the same stop, but it would be the same bus and also the same driver. While getting our bags out of the hold I said to the driver that it had been quite a trip up from Inverness. He agreed but said that the trip back down would be even worse. I thought he was just kidding around, but he wisnae.

Our first stop had to be *The Royal Hotel,* where we were staying that night. Fortunately it was just around the corner from where we got off the bus. I had checked out the area on my computer and knew exactly where to go.

It is a pretty standard looking old hotel with one of those revolving doors at the front. When you are carrying a rucksack and towing a small suitcase, these things become more of an obstacle course than an entrance way. I had visions of being stuck in there and having to be rescued.

I would have to say that the Royal has lost some of its former glory. You can see that the hotel had once been an up-market venue, but that was quite some time ago. We were given rooms on the second floor and took the lift up there.

That turned out to be a bit of an experience. It had to be the slowest lift I had ever been in. It was hard to tell if it was actually moving. It was also the only fully carpeted lift I have ever seen. I don't mean just the floor; the walls were carpeted as well.

As soon as I saw my room I was convinced that once again I had drawn the short straw. Whenever we go away anywhere it seems that John always gets the biggest and best room. For example I was on holiday in Tenerife with Irene and, for once, we were in a big fancy hotel. We had been there quite happily for a week when John and Kate arrived. Once we got a look at their room we realised our room was tiny by comparison. It was the size of the cleaner's equipment cupboard. I spent the next week expecting the jannie to arrive at our door looking for his mop and bucket. It turned out that I was right about my room in the Royal: it was half the size of John's.

We wanted to get out and get the metal detecting done as quickly as possible, so we just dumped our cases in our rooms, John in his suite and mine in my cupboard, and we headed out into Thurso.

Although we were keen to get onto the beach and start scanning we were also a wee bit thirsty, I had seen what looked like an old-fashioned pub quite close to the hotel. Things didn't turn out quite as planned however.

The *Y-Not Inn* really didn't sound like the kind of place we would like, so it was no great surprise when we didn't. I would imagine that if you belong to its target range of being between 18 and 35, earning quite a bit more than minimum wage and lacking in any real taste, The *Y-Not Inn* might appeal. Since none of the above applied to us we couldn't stand the place. It had the feel of an industrial building which had been converted into an entertainment centre. I think it could be described as clinical. Having a stainless steel bar didn't soften that effect.

The level of service we received did nothing to change our view of the place. There were two young girls behind the bar and we were the only customer standing there, yet we were totally ignored. It seems that both girls were in engaged in making one cup of coffee, and making heavy weather of it.

I could see that John was getting a bit angry about the lack of service, so I tried to defuse the situation. I suggested that maybe the girls hadn't been working behind the bar for very long and were still learning the ropes. He thought that there was a good chance that their bartending career had started about the same time as we got off the bus in Thurso.

If you've been inside, you'll know Y-Not

Dislike was replaced by shock when we discovered that our two drinks had cost us £9.00. At those prices there was no way we would be hanging around to see if the service improved.

We had both thought that the *Y-Not Inn* was a pretty stupid name for a pub, but, after trying it out, John thought it was quite apt, as long as you're allowed to say exactly why not. He had a long and descriptive list as to the reasons why punters should not go in there.

I had taken a little time to check out other pubs in the town and found a likely candidate for a visit. *The Commercial* sounded like a reasonable place for us to visit for a quick pint before hitting the beach. Fortunately that is what we found when we walked through the doors of The Comm. The differencces between this place and the one we had just left were considerable..

The Commercial Bar, Thurso

Just in the door we couldn't help but notice that there were quite a few people standing up at the bar, a couple of whom turned and nodded to us as we walked over to get served. The barmaid was waiting for us, with a smile on her face; things couldn't have been better. Actually that's not entirely true, the booze was still horrendously expensive. It turns out that spirits and mixers are much more expensive up north.

Barmaid Tina Williamson, was keen to find out what we were up to. We had been telling her about our long journey up to Thurso from Glasgow. When we told her what we intended doing on the beach, she did what everyone we meet does on hearing about us metal detecting; she laughed. The great thing is, after the initial mocking, most people admit that they wouldn't mind a wee shot at it themselves. While we were chatting I had to ask her where her accent was from, as it didn't sound entirely local. There was a good reason for that as she is originally from Kilwinning in Ayrshire. She has been living in Thurso for 20 years.

Tina, behind the bar in The Comm, Thurso

The three of us had a good laugh about our earlier choice of pub the *Y-Not Inn*, with Tina saying it would be the last pub she would have recommended to two auld yins like us. She did mention another pub we could try, but said that *The Comm* was our best bet for a decent pint and comfortable surroundings. Before we set off, at last, for the beach, Tina gave us directions to a very nice Chinese restaurant.

The beach was only 200 yards away and we were soon down on the sand with the detector doing its business. The pickings were a bit slim to start with. From the evidence we dug up, the particular spot we had chosen must have been rather popular with the kind of people who favour those throwaway barbecues.

After the third or fourth load of tinfoil John demanded that we move down near the waterline. The only problem with that was the giant seaweed barrier between us and the area he wanted to scan. I suggested a detour around the mass of thick, stinking weed, but he was having none of that and marched straight on. The dammed stuff was more than 6 inches deep. I was covered in it and the smell coming from it suggested that there was something other than seaweed involved.

Now that we were on firmer ground the detector seemed to be going off all the time. Being wet, the sand we were digging up wouldn't go through our sieve, making the search that much harder. We found absolutely nothing on this part of the beach, which was strange given all the signals we were getting.

It was only after a quarter of an hour of frustration that it suddenly dawned on me what was wrong. When we first got the detector I had read up on its use. It seems that sand which is saturated with seawater can give off rogue signals. It has something to do with all the minerals in the salt water. You would think he would have been grateful for this piece of information but no, instead John started ranting on about me wasting time.

There was nothing else for it but to wade back through the mountain of rotting seaweed and start all over again. It's really lucky that we did, because it was at that point that we made one of the best finds so far on our adventures. It doesn't usually take much to get John excited, but for once it was justified. The detector gave off a strong signal and to be honest I thought that maybe we had discovered an entire barbecue, but once John started digging it became obvious that we had found something more substantial.

I recognised it straight away; it was a film container, like a smaller version of the movie cans used to deliver feature films to your local picture house. Back in the 1970s I used to own an 8 mm camera and projector, so I consider myself a bit of an expert on the subject, compared to John anyway. I happen to know that the film for the really early 8 mm cameras was reversible. It was essentially a length of 16 mm film which came on 25 foot spools. After shooting the film, it would be taken out of the camera reversed and put back in to shoot the second 25 foot length. When it was developed it was split up the middle into two 25 foot lengths, then joined end to end to make a 50 foot 8 mm film. This might sound a bit complicated, but the point was, when bought, it came in at 16 mm film canister, just like the one we had found. I made the mistake of telling John this and I could instantly see his mind was racing to come up with one of his creative explanations. He came up with a real stoater. It seems that he had been reading a bit of history.

He was particularly interested in Scapa Flow, over on the Orkneys. As soon as he saw the old film tin he was convinced it was linked to the events of 1939 when HMS Royal Oak was sunk by German submarine in Scapa Flow. He insisted that finding this film canister so close to Orkney could only mean that it had come from a submarine which had been spying out the entrance to Scapa Flow before the attack was launched. I did point out that the writing on the tin seemed to be in English, but there was no stopping him.

Since it was unlikely that we would find anything else of the same historical importance I proposed that we pack up and head to a pub to celebrate.

Tina from *The Comm* had said that we might like *the Holborn Hotel* for a wee drink. The bar was a bit more modern than *the Comm*, but it was very comfortable and fairly busy for that time of the evening.

We didn't get a chance to talk to any of the bar staff but we got the impression that *the Holborn* was used by a slightly older clientele than the first pub we visited. It would have been quite easy to just sit back and enjoy a few more beers, but we really needed something to eat, so we headed back down to the hotel to drop off the detector before checking out the Chinese restaurant.

It must have been a bit too early for Thurso's diners, as we were the only customers. When you find yourself alone in a big restaurant it is hard not to think the worst. Maybe he locals knew something and were voting with their feet. To be honest we were too hungry to care, even when we found out what they were charging.

The waiter said our food would take about 40 minutes, presumably because the kitchen had just started up. That gave us time to sample a couple of bottles of exotic, and hugely over-priced, beer. Just to get a little value for money I made sure that we ate every crumb of those crispy prawn crackers that they leave on the table.

We had a simple plan for the remainder of the night. First we planned to revisit Tina round at *the Commercial*. After an unspecified number of beers we then intended to find the bar in our hotel, just to see how long they allowed residents to drink after last orders.

The Comm was a bit busier when we made our return. This time we entered via the lounge door. The mixed crowd in there was a fair bit younger than the old crowd in the bar, so we didn't hang around in there too long. Back in the bar we chatted to Tina for a while, telling her all about the stuff we had found on the beach. When John started repeating himself I realised that it was time to leave the poor girl in peace.

We finished our drinks and headed back to our hotel. Actually that was a bit of a risk on our part, as we had no real proof that there was a bar in our hotel.

On its website *The Royal* does claim to have a bar, but when we checked in, the bar, which is next to the main entrance, looked as if it has been shut for some time. The name above the door, MACNAB'S BAR BRASSERIE, looked fairly new, but there was absolutely no sign of any pub-related activity.

Now, as we approached it, at a time when any self-respecting boozer should be heaving with drunks, it still looked closed. However we are not that easily put off, so we went into the hotel and found a way through into the bar. It is a fairly large bar, which probably looked even bigger because it was more or less empty.

John holds court in the hotel bar

After ordering our drinks we got talking to the barman, James Murray and Colin Maddison the only other customer, who turned out to be the off duty manager of the hotel. James told us that the bar had once been one of the most popular in the town, but in recent years, trade had fallen away. That tends to be the way of things with pubs; they all seem to get their turn.

Colin told us that he was originally from Newcastle, but, to be perfectly honest, he really didn't need to. Apart from the accent, he was a dead ringer for Alan Shearer. It should of course be remembered that a fair amount of drink had been consumed by this time, and our ability to identify famous lookalikes might be a bit questionable. A wee while later our time-telling abilities also became impaired. I have no idea what time it was when we made our way up to our rooms, bringing to an end the first day of our longest ever trip.

We needed to catch the early bus down to Inverness so it was an early breakfast for us. John phoned me from his luxurious suite to tell me he was on his way down and would meet me outside my room.

I thought it might have been lingering effects of last night's booze, but the lift seemed to be going even slower than usual. It was only when it shook violently and we heard a loud bang that we both realised something had gone badly wrong.

Being trapped in a lift is never a good experience; being trapped in a lift with someone who has a tendency toward blind panic when under stress is the stuff of nightmares. John was pressing every available button, at such a rate that it sounded like he was sending out an SOS in Morse Code.

When the lift doors eventually opened, Colin, our Geordie pal from the night before was standing there. Maybe it was his professional calmness, or the fact that we were still half-cut from the night before, but when he said "you're in the basement; if you press number one, you will get back up to the dining room", we did just that. It was only much later on that day that it occurred to either of us that getting back onto a lift that had just plunged down the shaft, was just not sensible.

I had been under the impression that the hotel had been almost empty. Sitting in the huge, mostly empty, dining room just reinforced that idea. So I was more than a little surprised when what seemed like a couple of busloads of American tourists descended on the place. I was glad to see that the hotel was getting the trade but I couldn't help but wonder where they had all been the night before; they certainly weren't in the bar.

John: ***A review of the day.*** Apart from the terror of getting stuck in the lift, we had a great time in Thurso. Our find on the beach was astonishing (photo and description below). The pubs were mixed. *The Commercial Bar* was brilliant, some of the others not so. Prices are definitely more expensive up North.

Today' s finds;

John's thoughts on today's finds:

Our find today was amazing, and could turn out to have historical interest. As you can see from the photograph, the object seems to be the cover from a can of 8mm film. Now that in itself is not very exciting. Except when you think of where we found it and at what time was this film was in use.

For those readers who do not know, the beach at Thurso looks on to the Orkney Islands. The water separating them is the Pentland Firth, one of the most dangerous stretches of water in the world, and graveyard to many great ships.

A couple of years ago, Kate and I spent a few days with Kate's pal Sandra, and her husband Jim. They had a wee house, and a lot of land, in the St. Mary's area of Orkney. We travelled all over the island and saw some amazing sights. One of the most interesting things for me was the Churchill Barriers.

The background to the barriers is that in 1939, the Germans sneaked into Scapa Flow and sank The Royal Oak, one of Britain's greatest warships. To avoid a repeat of this, Churchill ordered the passageways into Scapa Flow to be blocked, leaving only one passageway open. This would make the bay more easily defended.

A wee bit of the horse and stable door tactic if you ask me. Anyway, the barriers were built in record time, with the help of Italian prisoners of war. They are magnificent structures and a great help today in getting round the islands.

As to how the Germans managed to sneak through one of the channels that were not thought to be navigable is a good question. Some people believe that they had been using submarines to sneak to the channels, surface in the early morning and film the approaches to work out the best way of getting in.

It is a fact, I think, that at least one of the submarines sank in the Pentland Firth in terrible weather. It is possible, aye, likely, that the vessel may have broken up. The lid of the film canister in the photograph could have come from that wreck. I know it is only my theory, but it could have happened. I'm sure Craig will give you a less romantic version of the source of the find.

While I was thinking about the Orkneys, I remembered that Kate and I visited the Italian Chapel, also built by the Italian prisoners of war. This is a beautiful building and well worth a visit. Beside it there is a small building from which locally produced wines and liqueurs are sold. We were so taken by the place that we purchased some of their products. A point of interest: The liqueurs are not too bad, but the wine is bowfin.

Craig's thoughts on today's finds

I think the film tin will prove very useful to us. It will give us somewhere to keep all the wee bits of rusty wire we are forever digging up.

Aberdeen

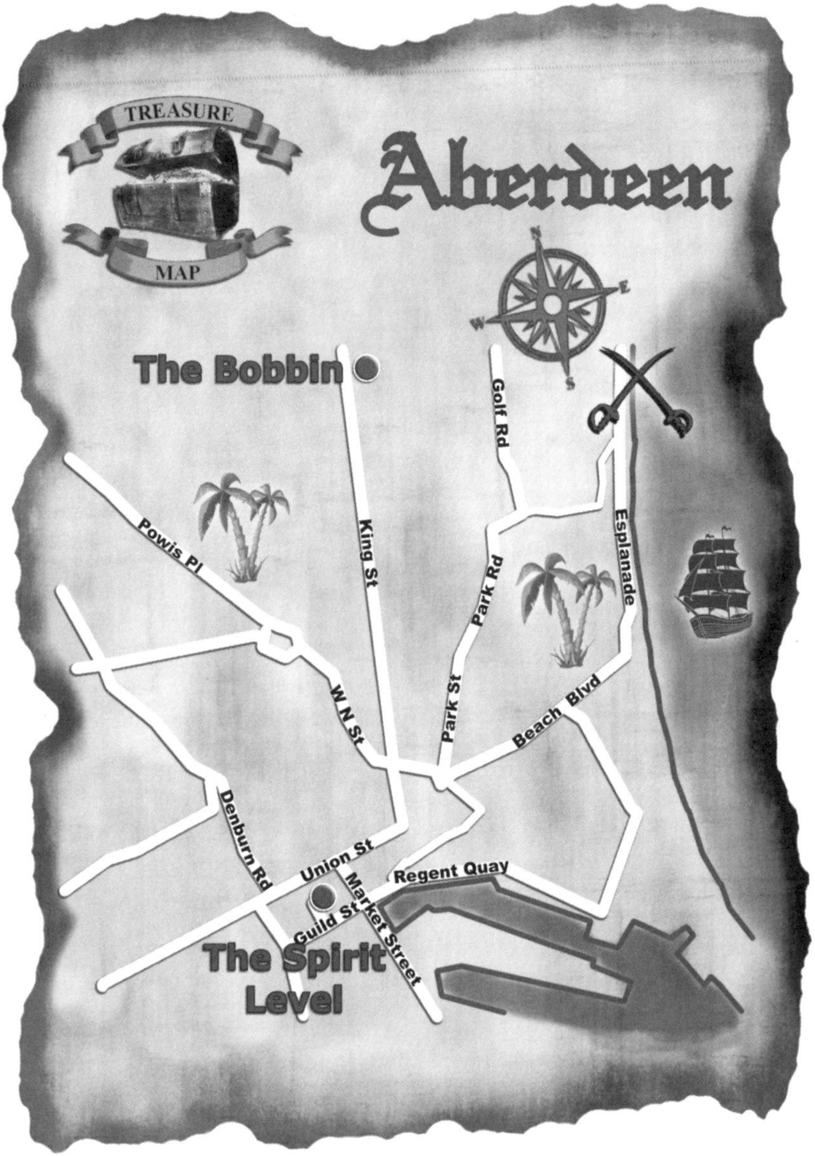

TREASURE
MAP
Aberdeen
N
E
W
S
The Bobbin
Golf Rd
Powis Pl
King St
Park Rd
Esplanade
W N St
Park St
Beach Blvd
Denburn Rd
Union St
Regent Quay
Market Street
Guild St
The Spirit Level

John: ***The journey.*** We had had a heavy night in Thurso and neither of us was at our best during breakfast. Things were not helped by the fact that the room was packed with American tourists who must have been on a bus tour round the North of Scotland. It's those tour parties that are keeping a lot of older hotels in Scotland in business.

Before we left the hotel, we had an incident in the lift. I'm sure Craig has explained.

It was a lovely morning as we boarded our bus, the same X99, with the same driver who brought us up from Inverness yesterday. It gave us confidence that he would know the way back.

When we got back to Inverness, we again had about an hour to kill before our Aberdeen bus. I was up for a pint, but Craig said he could not face one, and just wanted a cup of tea and a roll. This was about 11.30am on a Saturday morning, and we were free agents. It's the best time of the week for a wee sensation. But he was having none of it. He's getting old and bad tempered.

So we just went into the wee cafe at the station and Craig had a roll and sausage. It's hard to believe, but he was mad because it was not a square sliced sausage! I had the munchies, so had a plate of macaroni and chips. The chips were obviously reheats from yesterday. Craig said that reheated chips are called 'Backhet'. He claims it's a common term in Ayrshire, but was still disgusted that I managed to eat the lot.

When I booked the bus to Aberdeen, I didn't realise that on a Saturday, there's no X10 running, it's only a 10. This means that the bus visits every town and village between Inverness and Aberdeen, and takes about three and three quarters of an hour in the process. Thankfully, we both slept most of the way.

We had to get a bus from Aberdeen Bus Station to our wee B & B, but it took only about five minutes and dropped us right outside the door. We were warmly welcomed by our host and shown to our very nice rooms. It was time to see if we could repeat our beach success in Aberdeen.

Craig: ***The day's Beaches and Bars.*** I'm not sure if I was poisoned in Inverness or whether it was just a culture clash. In the cafe at the bus station I asked the girl behind the counter if I could have a roll and sausage. As anyone from Central Scotland will appreciate, what I was actually saying was, could I please have a large piece of square sausage in a roll. At no time did I opt for two large greasy links. I was back at our table before I realised what an awful mistake had been made. I had to eat the damned thing knowing full well that I would be getting regular reminders of it throughout the day and possibly well into the night.

On arrival in Aberdeen be made straight for our digs in King Street. Using the satnav on my phone we arrived at Lillian Guest House without a hitch. Almost immediately we experienced a hitch: we couldn't get in. After a few minutes ringing the bell, then banging on the door, I was beginning to think that John's plan was slowly unravelling. Just when I was working myself up for a good old rant about his organising abilities, a wee man appeared from the house next door.

It seems that, although the two houses have different names and numbers, they are owned by the same people. Once we booked in John asked the bloke if he had a really good room and, if so, could he give it to me. I would like to say that his conscience was bothering him about me always getting the worst room on offer, but I'm fairly sure that he was just sick of listening to me ranting on about it.

My room was on the ground floor and it really was rather good, four star quality perhaps. The only problem I could see was the set up in the bathroom. There was a full-length mirror on the back of the door. Why any designer would think that people using the facilities in there would like to admire themselves while doing so is beyond me. I try to avoid mirrors at the best of times; 5 o'clock in the morning with an upset stomach is not the best of times.

We decided to make a start on the detecting straight away. So, after dumping all our bags we set out towards Aberdeen beach. Actually there was one slight detour, we really needed a drink.

The Bobbin, just up the road from our digs on King Street, was sort of on our way, so we popped in for a quick one. From the outside *the Bobbin* looks to be a bit of a ramshackle; I liked it. Inside, however, it is ultra-modern, with lots of bright lights and terrible music; I didn't like it. The service left a lot to be desired as well. We were totally ignored for about 10 minutes, and even when we were eventually served it turned into a bit of a pantomime.

The Bobbin, Aberdeen

The young barmaid didn't seem quite up to the job. John ordered a vodka and soda for himself and a pint of lager for me. The girl said to him you mean a vodka and lemonade. No I didn't he replied but she was insistent. This went on for some time before she eventually gave up and filled him the drink he asked for. She then turned to me and asked me what I wanted to drink. I thought she was talking to somebody behind me at first, as I was standing there with my pint in my hand. She got the last laugh though as the round cost a fortune. Then again maybe she charged extra for lemonade.

It was a fair old walk from the pub down to the beach, and I was pretty knackered by the time we got there. After 10 minutes or so we got a hit on the detector. It turned out that we had found a stone. Not quite the start I was hoping for, but John seemed quite excited by it.

The lonely life of the metal detectorist

As usual we managed to attract the attention of some locals who were walking along the shore. I suspected that John had switched on his nutter magnet again as the two old ladies who came over to us were a little bit odd. They were walking their dog, and the poor wee thing didn't seem too keen. It was probably embarrassed. They had dressed it up in something which looked like a pink tutu. They asked all the usual questions but, to be honest, I couldn’t really concentrate for watching the poor wee mutt.

We kept scanning, without much luck, for another 10 minutes before the buzzer went again. This time we dug up a piece of wire. To me it looked like a bit of a coat hanger, but John disagreed. He was certain that it was some vital piece of equipment from a naval vessel. It amazes me that he thinks every single thing we find is important.

By the time we had finished the stretch of beach we were working I was in a bit of pain from my foot. John had noticed and he phoned for a taxi to get us back to the guesthouse. I thought that was a great idea, but also realised that I now owed him. He could now get up to any old nonsense and I wouldn't be able to tell anyone.

That night we headed into the city centre, intending to have a few beers and something to eat. To complete the first of these tasks, we visited our favourite Aberdeen pub, *The Spirit Level*. It was a bit noisier than we were used to, but then we had never visited it on a Saturday night before. We had been looking for Jackie and Julie, the licensees, but were told that neither of them were working that night. However, Julie's daughter was on duty behind the bar, and just like her 'maw' she had the bar running smoothly.

John asked her if she knew of a good chip shop nearby, but, unfortunately she didn't. Not to be beaten though she got her computer out to check online. Now that is what I call service.

The entertainment was just starting and it raised the sound level in the pub to a new ear splitting level. John, who was sitting with his back to the music, said to me that he thought the female singer was pretty good. I agreed with him, but had to point out that the singer was not actually a female. It was shaping up to be a rather strange night.

There was a hen party in, with a group of about 10 girls dressed in some very outlandish costumes. It was all getting a bit much for John, who was a bit shell shocked by the noise and the fashion choices of some of the customers.

Since we had failed to find a chip shop, we both decided to head back up to *The Bobbin* and get something to eat there. We took a taxi up the road and chatted to the driver on the way. He told us that Aberdeen was suffering badly due to the collapse of the oil industry: shops, pubs and of course taxis were all feeling the pinch.

I could tell that he was trying very hard to even out his own money problems, when he charged us £8.00 for a journey we could have done on foot, in about 20 minutes, sore foot notwithstanding.

Back in *The Bobbin*, we were told that the kitchen had closed just before we got there. After a couple of drinks we decided that the only thing left to us was a trip to the Co-op just up the road. We ended our Saturday night out sitting next to the kitchen in our guest house, eating sandwiches which were uncomfortably close to their sell by date. Boy do we know how to have a great night out on the town.

We were up bright and early the next morning, possibly because we were keen to get on or, more likely, because we had had so little to drink the previous night.

After a great breakfast, we got our bags and headed out to the bus stop, just a few feet away from the front door. Trying to get on the bus with my rucksack and case was even more difficult than usual. The bus we got was a single decker in name only. There was one double seat behind the driver, but the rest of the seats were up a flight of narrow stairs; I very nearly didn't make it.

Worse still, I think I hit my case off the shoulders of every passenger sitting on the outside seats. My apologies seemed to be falling on deaf ears as I smashed my way to the back of the bus. How people with mobility problems are supposed to use this bus is a mystery to me.

Thankfully the bus journey ended in the station, so I waited until everyone else got off. This made my exit much easier and, perhaps, quite a bit safer, since there was less opportunity for my victims to take their revenge.

We were a bit early for our second visit to *The Spirit Level*, as it was still half an hour until opening time. But by the time we had a coffee at the station, the shutters were being raised all over Aberdeen. Even at 11:05 we were not the first customers in the pub. That suggested to me that we were among friends. What better way to start off a Sunday than with a couple of pints.

Julie lifts our spirits

Julie spotted us as soon as we got through the door. I've lost count of the number of times we've been in this pub, but we have always had a great welcome. Over a couple of drinks we caught up with what had been going on since our last visit. At one point I happened to mention that we had enjoyed the entertainment in the pub the previous night. Julie said that the bloke who had been singing is very popular in Aberdeen with quite a following. I had been about to say that, while he was doing a medley of Queen's greatest hits, he had managed to out-camp Freddie Mercury, when she added, "of course he usually does a drag act, but I don't think that *The Spirit Level* is quite ready for that". John was heard to mutter something to the effect that he knew of at least two customers who certainly weren't ready for it.

A customer walked past at this time and Julie, without pausing for breath, shouted over, "You're looking better than you did the last time I saw you." The bloke asked her what she meant, and she replied, "Upright."

While we were chatting, John was checking out which vodkas were available in the pub and he spotted a bottle of Ketel One, his favourite brand. We have experience of this particular drink. A few books ago, we were in Falkirk when John saw a bottle of it on the gantry of the pub we were sitting in.

The sight of it made him come over all nostalgic. It seems that, in his working days, when he had to travel around America, Ketel One was his drink of choice. Back then however, he had a generous expense account. In Falkirk, as a special treat, I suggested that we try a wee hauf. I was stunned to find that two 25 ml measures cost £9.00.

In *The Spirit Level* I was about to tell him that our kitty couldn't stretch to such exotic booze, when Julie lifted the bottle over and sat it on the bar. She told us that nobody in her pub ever drank the stuff, so we may as well have it. Before I could turn down this kind offer, and let's face it, John wasn't about to do so, Julie sat two glasses down and poured a healthy measure into each. According to John, this vodka has to be taken neat. It really was good, but one was enough, any more and I think we would have been sitting down for a session, and probably ending our tour a bit early. As it was, we only just got back to the bus station in time for a connection to Montrose.

At the bus station John had announced that he wanted to sit upstairs and at the front of the bus. He said that he wanted a panoramic view of the wonderful scenery on the road down to Montrose. Needless to say he was asleep before the bus left the station.

John: ***A review of the day.*** After our long journey down from Thurso, we had a quick pint in *The Bobbin* before we walked, very slowly, down to the beach. Craig's feet were not too good. But we got there and enjoyed our detecting.

The view from the beach of about 20 or so big support vessels moored was the visual proof of the tremendous effect the the downturn in the oil business is having on everybody in the town. All the bar staff and taxi drivers we spoke to are worried about the effect this is having on the town.

Our night out was a lot quieter than in Thurso, and after a few pints in a couple of bars, we were back in our digs at the back of eleven.

John's thoughts on today's finds:

It was going to be hard to repeat yesterdays success, and so it turned out. But one of our finds, the metal wire, although not looking like anything special, is likely to be a piece of the wire that joins one part of a ship's engine to another. You could feel the history when you held it. The other find was a piece of metal oxide contained in a black stone. Every find, no matter how small, or insignificant it may seem, is important.

Craig's thoughts on today's finds

Whatever was found on the beach today clearly wasn't up to much,

Montrose

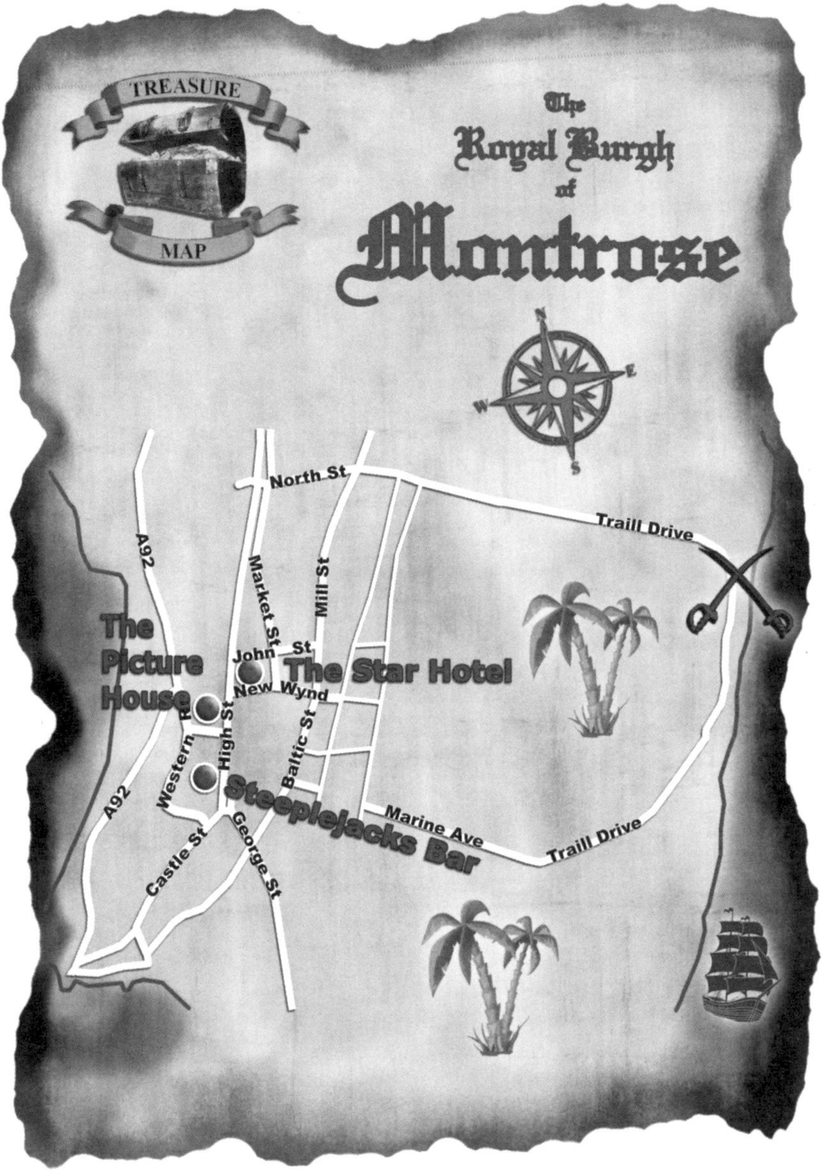
TREASURE
MAP
The Royal Burgh of Montrose
N
E
W
S
North St
Traill Drive
A92
Market St
Mill St
The Picture House
John St
The Star Hotel
New Wynd
Western Rd
High St
Baltic St
Steeplejacks Bar
Marine Ave
Traill Drive
A92
Castle St
George St

John; *The journey*: We met for breakfast feeling refreshed and ready to get pissed again. A relatively quiet night had us back to the fore.

I had a feeling we were going to have a great day. We got the local bus into Union Street, and after a cup of coffee, taken only to kill the time till the eleven o'clock opening hour, we headed back into our favourite bar in Aberdeen, *The Spirit Level.*

Our journey down to Montrose on the X7 was enjoyable. We sat upstairs at the front and watched the East Coast scenery fly by us. About an hour later we were getting off the bus just round the corner from our next wee overnight, *The Star Hotel,* and what a great hotel it turned out to be.

When we booked in, the owner said that he had upgraded us from the basic rooms I had booked to superior ones. He failed to mention that the upgraded rooms were up on the third floor, and there was no lift. Not that we would have used it after our experience in Thurso. Craig was knackered by the time we got up the three flights. But we were in Montrose, ready to dig and party.

Craig's Beaches and Bars*:* We found our hotel in Montrose very quickly, mainly due to my keen sense of direction and my magic phone. *The Star Hotel* is to be found just off High Street, in New Wynd.

There is no big sign on the front of the place displaying the hotels name, but, fortunately for us, there was a large red Tennent's sign on the wall. This particular sign acts like a magnet on us, dragging us towards the promise of a nice cold beer and good company. And that's exactly what we got in *The Star.*

Unusually, for a hotel, *The Star* has no reception area to negotiate when entering the building. Instead you step straight into the bar.

To me this is a much more civilised way of dealing with customers. As soon as we got in the door some of the regulars came over to talk to us. Before we checked in we thought it would be a good idea to check out the booze. Our barmaid, Sarena Alexander, served up the drinks and, I'm glad to say, the lager and the vodka both passed the test.

Considering some of the prices we had been paying, the drink in *The Star* was so cheap that John thought he had died and gone to heaven, which would have been a possibility if we were to stay there too long.

David Bray, the hotel owner, came over to give us some good news - we had been upgraded. Unfortunately, for my sore feet, we had been upgraded to the top of the hotel. By the time we got to the top of the stairs I was ready to drop. I did notice that there was a nice big armchair sitting outside my room, and could imagine that I would probably make good use of it, if I had to climb the stairs too often that day.

Sarena Alexander and David Bray (gaffer)

Back down in the bar we talked to some of the other customers. One of them seemed particularly interested in our metal detecting activities. Being a bit of a self-taught expert, I took it upon myself to explain the techniques and principles behind the science of metal detecting. I was wishing the floor would open up when our new friend, Jim, explained that he had been in the army, and had specialised in mine detecting. He had been in the 1st Battalion of the Scots Guards as part of a pioneer warfare group, at least I think that's what he said as I was still in shock.

He told us that the mine detectors they were using in the early 70s were pretty much useless; most of the time the only things they would pick were old rusty nails. I was about to say that I knew how that felt, but given what he was trying to find, I decided that wandering about a beach for a couple of hours wasn't quite in the same league.

Jim, mine detector. John, mental detector

Jim had seen action in Northern Ireland and had come under fire a few times. He told us that one of his squad was wounded in one incident. He started laughing at this point, and I had to ask him what could possibly be funny about someone being wounded. He said that the soldier was still lying in the road when the ambulance arrived. The medic jumped out and asked him if there was anything they could do for him. The squaddie, who wasn't too badly wounded, said "You could get your Land Rover off my hand." In their hurry to help, they had parked their vehicle on his outstretched hand.

The drink was flowing by this time and we realised that if we didn't get down to the beach pretty soon we were likely never to see it.

It is a fair stroll down to the beach, and we were aware that the weather, which had been good up until then, was taking a turn for the worse. Working quickly, we assembled the machine and started scanning. Within a few minutes we came across one of the biggest objects we have ever found. John was struggling to get it out of the ground as it was fairly heavy. I would have given him a hand, but I see myself as more of a technician than a labourer, so I left him to it.

The object itself seemed to be part of a chain and of course John had a theory. Since I had no idea what the thing could be, I had to admit that for once he might be right. He was delighted, and to celebrate he suggested that we go back to the hotel for a drink. The rain was stoating down by the time we got back to the bar.

I volunteered to take the detector up to my room, while John volunteered to check the gantry for any signs of exotic vodkas. At the top of the stairs I eyed up the big armchair, but managed to get into my room before collapsing on the bed.

When I got back downstairs I found John in deep conversation with David, *The Star's* owner. They were talking football, a language I never really learned. It seems that David was once Crystal Palace's scout in Scotland. Hearing this led to much discussion about the future of Scottish football, and led me to concentrate on my drinking.

The staff behind the bar had changed while we were out detecting. David Proctor was now filling the glasses and dispensing a little local history. He told us that *The Star* had not always been the great bar it is now. In his time behind the bar he had seen a few rough nights. Bar room brawls were not unheard of. In fact the hotel had the unenviable nickname of The Stab Inn. All of that changed when David Bray took over. *The Star Hotel* is now definitely on the up.

Although we would have been quite happy just to stay where we were, it was time to get something to eat. Fiona MacGregor, the other half of the bartending team, suggested that we go over to *the Picture House.*

Davie Proctor behind the bar in the Star

Obviously I thought that she was trying to get rid of us but, she explained that she wasn't suggesting that we quit drinking and take in a movie instead. *The Picture House* she was talking about was, in fact, a bar restaurant. That made all the difference.

As soon as Fiona explained that to us, I remembered our last visit to Montrose, when we had in fact visited *the Picture House.* Back then I distinctly remember that we were not impressed. That being said, at that time food was the furthest thing from our minds. We were on a quest to find really good boozers, and that place did not score many points in that department.

Before making our way over there I asked Davy if he could recommend another pub to us, just for a bit contrast. He immediately came up with *Steeplejacks Bar.* He said it was not like any other pub in Montrose: he wasn't wrong

Our first stop however, was *The Picture House*, and it was exactly as I remembered it: more like a giant café than a pub. This time around I was quite happy with that. After much thought, we both ordered fish and chips, with two lager chasers. When our food arrived I couldn't believe the size of the fish - it had to be the biggest piece of haddock that I'd ever seen.

It occurred to me that sitting in this building having fish and chips was quite ironic. Many years ago when I was a lad I was thrown out of a picture house in Kilmarnock for eating a fish supper. I was about to share this moment of irony with John, when I realised that first I would have to explain to him what irony was. Since we only had an hour to spare I decided not to bother.

The food was really good and the beer was more than passable, so I take back any bad stuff I might have said about the place on a previous visit.

Steeplejacks Bar was just a short walk along High Street. Looking at the front of the pub it would appear to be the smallest bar in Scotland. But fortunately it opens up once you pass along the corridor from the front door. When we managed to reach the bar, we were confronted by what John described as 'a scene from the bar in Star Wars'. Groups of people were dancing away to some pretty dodgy 60s music. That was quite apt really, as the decor of the place suggested the same time period. This was only the second real bar we had been visited in Montrose, and once again the locals were very friendly. Everyone seemed willing to chat and share a laugh, so much so that we were both asked up to dance. I managed to avoid having to do so by claiming to have a bad back. John was not so fortunate. A big wummin grabbed him and, going by the look on his face, he was too feart to say no.

We had a couple of drinks at the bar and talked to the barmaid. I'm pretty sure John wrote her name down, but between the vodka swigging and the acrobatics on the dance floor, his notebook disappeared. Anyway, we had a fine old time in *Steeplejacks* and promised to pay another visit next time we found ourselves in Montrose.

Strictly X certificate in Steeplejacks

It was time for a nightcap back down in *The Star*, although, as it turned out, that nightcap turned into two or three. *The Star* was a bit busier by the time we got back there. A large group of young girls were making their presence known. The jukebox was blasting out some passable music, and everyone seemed to be enjoying themselves.

It was at this point that David, the owner, very nearly put an end to my slice of the enjoyment. He shouted over to the girls, telling them that we were in Montrose to write a book. If he had left it at that, things would have been just fine, but he followed that up by telling them that we had written about some of the town's bars in a previous book. That certainly set the cat among the pigeons. One of the girls shouted over, "You're the ones who wrote about *the Market Bar*. You said it was a dump and the service was terrible". Personally I don't remember using those exact words, but it was hard to deny that we had given the pub a bit of a slagging. Unfortunately the young lady wasn't quite finished with us. "I was working in there at the time you came in", she roared. The rest of the girls were howling and laughing by this time. I was beginning to panic a wee bit, thinking that we were about to get a real ear bashing, or possibly just a bashing.

Ashley Starrs, Lauren Lambert, Tracey Brake, Stephanie Brannan, Katie Mercer, Sarah Grant

John did exactly what I expected of him, he told them that it was me, and me alone who has written about the pub. He is nothing if not dependable. Fortunately, for the both of us, because if I was going down I was dammed sure that I would be taking him with me, the girl was only having a laugh at our expense. She said that we were right, the place was a dump. That certainly lightened the mood.

Just to keep things going we told them some of the dafter stories from previous adventures. As the night wore on the girls started dancing, which caused John a bit of concern. I think he was still a bit traumatised from his earlier grappling over at **Steeplejacks** and was keen to avoid a recurrence. That was the only possible reason for him to take over the jukebox. I think he played every undanceable tune in the thing.

The girls persuade me to write only good things about The Star Hotel

The remainder of the night is a bit blurry, but I assume we made use of our resident status to stay in the bar well beyond closing time. I'm just amazed that we made it up those stairs.

Breakfast was rather a quiet affair the next morning. I think that I might have managed a cup of tea and half a slice of toast, but I'm sure the full Scottish breakfast would have been delicious. We didn't have to leave till about 12 o'clock so I used the extra time wisely; I fell asleep on the big chair outside my room.

John: ***A review of the day:*** We had a great day on the beach and in the bars in Montrose. Any doubts we had about the place after a visit years ago were dispersed. The locals of both sexes are crazy (in a good way). When we eventually got to bed, we felt no pain. I have no idea how late it was, but it was late.

Today' s finds;

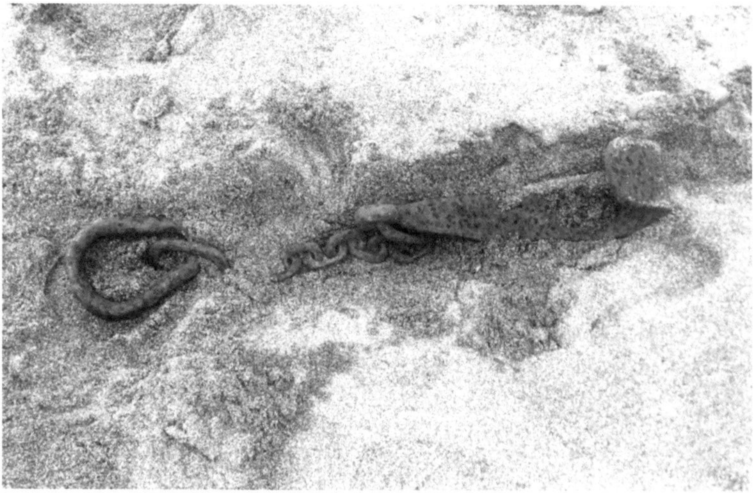

John's thoughts on today's finds:

Just when we thought that our find in Thurso would not be matched, wham, we did it again. Our *Garrett Ace 150* went mad after about 15 minutes of sweeping, and it took all our strength to pull out of its hiding place a giant chain with a very interesting curved end piece. I have no idea what exactly it is, but if I had to guess, and that's what I always do, I believe it’s some sort of link to an Anchor Chain, from a bloody big ship. But what do you think?

Craig's thoughts on today's finds

This was possibly the biggest find we have made. It is certainly the heaviest. I don’t really know what it was or what it was used for but, it must have been fairly important.

Carnoustie

TREASURE
MAP
Carnoustie
N
E
W
S
Maule St
Carlogie Rd
Queen St
Arbroath Rd
Church St
Ireland St
Station Rd
Dundee St
Station Hotel
Tayside St
Taymouth St
Links Parade
Carnoustie Bay

John; *The journey*: Montrose to Carnoustie is not too far a journey, but for the bus journey lover like me, it is nice to change buses on the way and visit another town. This was the case today.

After saying goodbye to David, we wandered round into High Street and got our No. 30 bus for the 26 minute journey down the coast to Arbroath Bus Station. I had a wee problem getting on the bus. I think the driver was French, and as I tried to give him my bus pass, he kept telling me something. It was Craig, with his limited French vocabulary, who told me that he was saying that there is a conductor on board. Right away I remembered that this had happened to me before in Dundee, when the driver was a local, and he told me that there was a conductor on the bus. I thought he was saying that the bus was going to Conductorin. I never learn!

Once we sat down and Craig stopped laughing, we had a lovely run to Arbroath. An interesting thing about the Arbroath Bus Station is that it is very big for the size of the place. It must have at least 10 bays.

After we got to our stance, we had about 20 minutes to kill, and I remembered that Arbroath was famous for the Arbroath Smokie, a dish which the good lady loves. When I asked Craig if I should nick round the corner and buy one, he reminded me of the last time I did this. The shrink wrapping didn't do its job properly, and the whole bus ended up honking. She would just have to make do with a fish supper!

Our No. 73 left on time, and after another lovely run down the East Coast in bright sunshine, we arrived in Carnoustie at 11.20am. Again, this is the best time of the day for a couple of pints to get you going, but for the second time in our four day trip, Craig could not face a pint. He'll have to go.

This was a pity, because Craig had used Google and found *the Station Hotel*, which was just round the corner from the bus stop and next to the railway line and the beach. The bar was very posh, not the kind we usually take to but, for some reason, I really liked the bar, and the hotel.

The two girls behind the bar, Rose and Rebecca, were great company, and even suggested that we leave our bags with them while we went down to the beach. I had a couple of pints and Craig had a Diet Coke then a cup of tea. If this was the other way round, I would have got dog's abuse from him. If he gets any worse, I might as well go drinking with a Jehova's Witness.

I normally let Craig give you the details of our time spent on the beach detecting, but since he spent almost the whole time with his head in his hands at a bench, I will do the report.

It was a glorious day, and with the excitement of our two good finds still fresh in my mind, I set about exploring the beach with vigour. Alas, as is usual, after the ups come the downs. Don't get me wrong, I found two pieces of Quartz-like stone, which you can see in the photograph below. After about an hour, I gave up and wakened Craig, and we wandered back up to the *Railway Hotel.*

Craig had recovered some of his sparkle, and even managed a pint with me before we left to get our bus into Dundee to start our journey home.

Craig: ***The day's Beaches and Bars.*** For someone who dislikes golf as much as I do Carnoustie might seem like an odd choice of a place to visit. I've never been there and never had any wish to go there. In fact going there with John, of all people, was downright strange. The man has a hundred boring stories to tell about his experiences in every major golf course in Scotland. I know this, because he has tormented me with his constant retelling of them, every time one of them it is mentioned in the paper or television, or even just in the passing by people who soon wish they hadn't. The only reason for choosing Carnoustie was that it is on the way home. To make the most of our road trip we needed to use the last day of our travels, and Carnoustie has a particularly fine sandy beach, as I found out from checking satellite pictures of the coast between Montrose and Dundee.

As ever we headed to the pub nearest the beach. In this case that was *The Station Hotel*. It wasn't too much of a walk down to the hotel. But the nearer we got to it, the more worried John became. We could see the door to the bar from some distance away and it looked securely closed. Since I had chosen this pub I knew that if that turned out to be the case I was in for some severe slagging. Just when things were looking really bad, we saw someone emerge from another door. It was the main entrance to the hotel and once inside we spied the lounge bar. It's a very traditional bar, perhaps a wee bit dull, but very comfortable.

The Station Hotel, Carnoustie

After getting settled on our bar stools, John ordered our drinks. However, I had to change that order. For the last four days, being keeper of the kitty, John has been ordering vodka and soda and a pint of lager at regular intervals; some might say far too regular. And that is where my problem lay. The previous night had been a particularly heavy one at the bar and, when you add in the cumulative effect of Thurso and Aberdeen, I was feeling like a change. John nearly fell over backwards when I put in my order: a cup of tea, two sugars no milk. Once he had regained his balance and stopped laughing, we introduced ourselves to the two barmaids. Rose Morgan and Rebecca Finan have been working in the Station for a while but, they had to admit that they had never had any metal detectorists in their bar before.

I took this as a good sign. Hopefully that meant that there was treasure to be found on Carnoustie's untouched beach. Rose and Rebecca were not convinced that we would find anything other than sand down there.

Rose and Rebecca in The Station Hotel, Carnoustie

John was really taken with this hotel and asked the girls how much a night's stay would cost him. I don't actually remember the figure mentioned, but I think it was fairly reasonable. However, when he asked what the going rate would be during the Open, they just laughed. I got the impression that you could probably buy a small car for the price of a room during such a high profile competition.

It was time to get some work done, so we started getting our bags arranged. When I told the girls that we would be back in before catching our bus, Rebecca suggested that we leave our bags behind and they would look after them for us. That was very kind of them and we accepted the offer.

Outside we watched the railway crossing barriers going up and down for the trains which sped past. It was really exciting; we don't have these kinds of crossings where we live. I think we must have been grinning like a couple of daft schoolboys. Any passing locals must have thought we were just down from the hill country. Once we tired of watching the barrier in action, we moved on to the beach. I managed to scan for about five minutes, before I had to give up. The sand was so soft it kept giving way under my foot. I was already getting a fair bit of pain from my foot anyway, but that just made it so much worse.

There was nothing else for it but to hand over the detector to John and make my way off the beach. As soon as I got back up to the grass everything was fine again. I decided to keep it that way by staying up there. John was quite happy to remain on the beach on his own, so I found a picnic table with a clear view of the crossing barriers and settled down to be entertained by them. I had no idea so many trains passed through Carnoustie.

I was enjoying the novelty of watching the flashing lights and listening to the warning hooter when it occurred to me that the locals probably saw the situation differently.

After about half an hour watching the trains go back and forth I suddenly remembered that the bottle of vodka we had been given by Julie up in Aberdeen was still in the equipment bag down on the beach. I'm not normally a suspicious person, but John had volunteered to stay on the beach all alone, just a little too readily.

Purely out of curiosity I snuck over to the long grass just above the beach. When I looked over the grass I was just in time to catch John taking a good swig out of the bottle. He claimed that he had only done this once, but I thought that it was highly unlikely that I had managed to catch him that one time. It serves me right - I should have put a mark on the bottle. Not long after I caught him, John decided that it was time to finish up on the beach and head back to the hotel.

I was feeling a bit better by the time we got there so, when John asked what I wanted to drink, I asked for a pint of lager. It was possible that the sea air had revived me, but it is equally possible that I was making sure that I got my share of the kitty.

Whatever the reason, the lager also worked it's magic, so much so that I had another one. While we were at the beach the girls had taken our bags and put them behind the desk at reception. We picked them up there and made our way back up to High Street to wait for a bus into Dundee. There was not enough time to take in the sights of Dundee, and by that I mean go to a pub. So John had to settle for a visit to the bus station café. I'm not a great fan of this place; the last time we had been in there we paid premium prices for some decidedly substandard food. But, since time was against us, we had no other option if we wanted something to eat.

I ordered a couple of cheese rolls and a biscuit, while John had two rolls and cold meat, a biscuit and a portion of chips. The chips were not quite ready, but John was determined to wait for them.

When we were told how much food was to cost us, we did what we do best, i.e. complained loudly. The bloke behind the counter said there is nothing he could do about the price, but, by way of compensation be chucked a couple of bananas into our paper bag.

We very nearly missed the bus waiting for those damn chips. Even when he did get them, he took ages trying to hide them in the inside pocket of his jacket.

For obvious reasons, ones that became all too obvious a few minutes after we left the station, bus companies frown on people bringing hot food on board their buses. Incidentally I only ate one of my rolls, the cheese had no actual taste. Furthermore, John’s chips, going by the taste of them, might not have contained any actual potato, and could well have been cooked in engine oil. Needless to say, he ate every one of them.

Our longest ever trip was over, thank God, and we had visited not only some great Scottish beaches but some really exceptional pubs. But best of all, we met some really great characters.

John: A review of the day: There is not much I can add to what I have already told you above. I really enjoyed today's journey. It is an area I have never been before, and is well worth a return visit. Carnoustie is a lovely wee place and both *The Railway Hotel* and the beach are well worth a visit.

Journeys home from a holiday of any kind are not as exciting as the start of the holiday. And this was the case today. We were both tired from four hard days’ work! Who am I kidding!

We both dozed on the No. 73 into Dundee. In the bus station we got some pieces and a bag of chips. Our M9 bus turned up right on time and we had to smuggle the chips on board; they were great and smelled the bus out.

After consuming our pieces and chips as quickly as possible in case we got thrown off the bus, we fell asleep and wakened refreshed in Buchanan Street Bus Station.

We got off the bus at about five past seven, went out of the bus station and got the wee bus that goes round from the Bus Station to Glasgow Central and Queen Street. It only took about two minutes, and we managed to get the 7.18pm train to EK. Mind you, we had to do our impersonation of running from the ticket office up to platform 11. We were last on and exhausted. Craig couldn't talk until we were at Clarkston.

So ended our epic four day, four beach, three night journey.

Will we do a similar thing again? I doubt it, but it was fun, and we met some great people and visited some wonderful, and strange places. Our finds were also amazing, and I am sure some of them will turn out to be history changers.

Might as well finish the book off with some real bullshit!

Today' s finds;

John's thoughts on today's finds:

Not our most exciting find, and similar to the type of valuable stones we have uncovered before. But a find is a find, and I am the one who is proud of finding it.

Craig's thoughts on today's finds

We have now found enough stones to allow us to build a reasonable sized dry-stane dyke.